Let's Talk: *50 Daily Devotionals*

BASED ON THE BOOK

I Am Jesus:
Let's Change
the World

Let's
Talk

50 Daily Devotionals

MY **EXCEPTIONAL** FOLLOWERS

MAKE AN **EXPONENTIAL** CHURCH

ELMER L. TOWNS

Author of *I Am Jesus: Let's Chance the World*

DESTINY IMAGE® PUBLISHERS, INC.
P.O. Box 310, Shippensburg, PA 17257-0310
"Promoting Inspired Lives."

This book and all other Destiny Image and Destiny Image Fiction books are available at Christian bookstores and distributors worldwide.

For more information on foreign distributors, call 717-532-3040.
Or reach us on the Internet: www.destinyimage.com

Cover and Interior Design by
Rob Williams, InsideOut Creative Arts
insideoutcreativearts.com

ISBN 13: TP 978-0-7684-4988-4
ISBN 13 Ebook: 978-0-7684-4989-1
For Worldwide Distribution, Printed in the U.S.A.
1 2 3 4 5 6 7 8 9 10 11 / 22 21 20 19 18

CONTENTS

I AM JESUS: LET'S CHANGE THE WORLD
ADVANCE READER SAMPLE

PART ONE
I AM JESUS: LET'S CHANGE THE WORLD

INTRODUCTION

Follow Me. I am Jesus. When you follow Me with all your heart, mind, soul and body, you will become an exceptional Christian. What does the word *exceptional* mean? It means you are extraordinary, or remarkable, or unexpected. I want to make you an outstanding believer. That is what I do; I asked fishermen to follow Me and they became fishers of people—evangelists—who won multitudes to salvation. Think of Peter's preaching at Pentecost; over 3,000 were added to the church (Acts 3:4), and after his next sermon there were 5,000 men added to the church (Acts 4:4). That meant family heads were added to the church, including their wives and children. Some have estimated over 20,000 followers.

They became exceptional followers; you can become an exceptional follower also. What must you do? Talk to Me in prayer in the next 50 days. First, I will explain the Scriptures to you and how you can become exceptional. Then you will tell Me your needs and desires. We will have a conversation—talking to each other. You can become far more exceptional than you ever dreamed.

That doesn't mean you will be perfect, but you can become an exceptional worshiper; that is where it all begins. Then you will become an exceptional intercessor, asking Me to do extraordinary works through you. Then you will become an exceptional witness to both the saved and the lost. The results can be extraordinary.

When you follow Me, you will be baptized into a local body of Christ called the local church. You can influence them as they influence you. Together with them, your church can have exponential results. The word *exponential* means the church is a living, growing body rapidly increasing in all areas according to a predetermined formula.

What's an exponential church? Its formula is motivated by My Great Commission, charged with preaching the gospel to everyone in the world. Will you help Me do that? The next 50 days of devotions will illustrate how the original Jerusalem church grew exponentially in every area. It saturated its city, then the surrounding area of Judea. Next it reached out to Samaria, a culture different from its own.

Then My church in Antioch sent out missionaries until the entire Roman Empire was saturated with the gospel. Now I want you to join in that crusade. I want you and all My followers in your church to become exponential witnesses.

Each of the next 7 weeks is divided into 7 daily devotions. The devotions for each week will help you and your church to become exceptional in character so that your church will become exponential in method and service.

WEEK 1 | I Am Jesus—A Church Growing Exponentially

WEEK 2 | I Am Jesus—A Revived Church

WEEK 3 | I Am Jesus—A Witnessing Church

WEEK 4 | I Am Jesus—A Teaching Church

WEEK 5 | I Am Jesus—A Ministering and Serving Church

WEEK 6 | I Am Jesus—My Church Expectations

WEEK 7 | I Am Jesus—Pictures of My Exponential Church

WEEK ONE

I AM JESUS:
A Church Growing Exponentially

The New Testament church is vastly different from the Old Testament sacrificial system and Jewish laws. The church was new, refreshing, freeing, and God the Father placed the life of the Holy Spirit in it. But most important, the church is Me, the body of Christ. I am Jesus living in My people and touching the world through My people. This week your reading and praying will focus on what I do for My people and for My church. When you properly know Me, you will strive to become an exceptional follower. What are the results? Many exceptional followers can build an exponential church.

I AM JESUS—*Be an Exceptional Believer*

"But you will receive power when the Holy Spirit comes upon you. And you will be my witnesses, telling people about me everywhere—in Jerusalem, throughout Judea, in Samaria, and to the ends of the earth."

ACTS 1:8, *NLT*

I am Jesus who calls you to a life of exceptional character. The word *exceptional* means you are extraordinary, remarkable, and unexpected. Don't live the way you lived before you began following Me. Reach higher, become more than you ever thought you could become: "If any person is in Me, they are a new creature" (2 Cor. 5:17, *BBJ*). I want to create you to be a remarkable worshiper, so you worship the Father in spirit (Holy Spirit) and truth (scripture). I want you to become a remarkable testimony to the saved and lost. When they look at you, I want them to see Me and be drawn to salvation. I want you to grow extraordinary faith—faith to move mountains (Mark 11:22-24). I want you to believe that I exist (Heb. 11:6), and that I will do remarkable ministries through you.

Lord, in my flesh I see my weaknesses and failures. Fill me with Your presence, give me a burden for ministry, direct me to the place You choose for me to serve. Then use me. Amen.

I am Jesus, who wants you and your church to be exceptional. Then you will see exponential results. The word *exponential* means explosion of growth according to My Great Commission. If you are exceptional in character, then I will use you in exponential ways. So learn, grow, worship, serve, and follow Me all the way, every day.

I have decided to follow You. I will be what you want me to be. I will go where You want me to go. I will do what You tell me to do. My commitment is for all my life, for all the days of my life. Amen.

READING: Acts 8:1-40

KEY THOUGHT: I want you to be My exceptional follower, so I can do exceptional ministry through you.

Day 2

I AM JESUS—*Be an Exponential Church*

*"But you will receive power when the Holy Spirit comes upon you.
And you will be my witnesses, telling people about me everywhere—in Jerusalem,
throughout Judea, in Samaria, and to the ends of the earth."*

ACTS 1:8, *NLT*

My church should be *exponential* in every way. The word exponential means rapid increase in all areas according to a predetermined formula. I gave the Great Commission as a predetermined strategy to get the gospel to all lost people. The power to get it done is in the Holy Spirit. The motive is love—I love all lost people: "The love of Christ constrains (you) . . . because (I) died for all" (2 Cor. 5:14-15, ELT). Also remember I said, "The works that I do (you) shall do also, and greater works" (John 14:12). What is greater than physical healing and turning 5 loaves and 2 fish into enough to feed 5,000? I tell you—its winning one hell-bound sinner to salvation, or even better, winning a whole church to salvation and getting them exponentially aggressive to reach their neighborhood—then planting another church in another unevangelized area.

Lord, forgive my sinful negligence. I will get serious about sharing my faith with family and friends. Help me see their lost condition and give me a boldness to win them to salvation. Amen.

Exponential means increased effort motivated by the Holy Spirit. The bottom line is not just a foreign missions program, or techniques, or methods. It is being personally energized to exponential fasting and prayer. That will lead to exponential giving that will led to exponential evangelism that results in exponential blessings. What's another word for exponential? Revival! Revival is My pouring My presence on My people. Do you need reviving?

*Lord, revive my spirit. I pray but need more fervency.
I serve but need more fruitfulness. Drops of mercy are falling around me,
but I ask for revival showers. Amen.*

READING: Mark 16:14-20; Acts 1:1-11

KEY THOUGHT: The greatness of the Great Commission demands our total commitment and energy to complete the task.

11

I AM JESUS—A Church Praying

"Stay here in the city until the Holy Spirit comes and fills you with power."
LUKE 24:49, *NLT*

"Then they all prayed . . . all the believers were meeting together in one place,
suddenly . . . everyone present was filled with the Holy Spirit."
ACTS 1:24; 2:1, 4

I am Jesus the church gathered for prayer—exponential prayer. Not just another group prayer meeting, but a time of confessing sin, admitting your failures, begging for spiritual power and faith to believe the Holy Spirit will come to fill with zeal and soul-winning evangelism. The early church prayed with boldness (Acts 4:29), and the room was shaken. Ultimately they were accused of "turning the world upside down" (Acts 17:6). What does that mean? The gospel transforms people and they changed their life and family. When that is added to a whole church, a neighborhood is turned upside down. Do you believe the church can change the world? Since I indwell a person (Gal. 2:20), let Me shine through you into your family and world.

Fill me with the Holy Spirit and revive me, so my testimony can revive my church
and change my world. Amen.

I am Jesus who promised "if you ask anything in My name, I will do it" (John 14:14, *NKJV*). So what is on your prayer list? Are you praying for lost family members to be saved? Have you prayed for opportunities to witness to them, to get them under the gospel preaching? Everything in your walk with Me begins with prayer. First, pray to know Me. Then pray to be filled with great faith; and third, pray to be an aggressive soul winner. Ask for revival in your church—then people will get saved: "You do not have because you do not ask" (Jas. 4:2, *NKJV*).

Lord, teach me to pray with bigger faith to expect You to do more in my family
and church. Teach me to pray for bigger results in evangelism. Lord, give me a
bigger burden to worship and serve You in all I do. Amen.

READING: Acts 4:1-31

KEY THOUGHT: The Great Commission expects great results in your church, so you and all in the church must give yourselves to great prayer.

I AM JESUS—*Exponential Faith*

"Jesus said to them . . . 'If you had faith even as small as a mustard seed,
you could say to this mountain, move from here to there, and it would move.
This happens only with prayer and fasting.'"

MATTHEW 17:20-21, ELT

I am Jesus, the Church body (Eph. 1:22-23). When two or three come together for prayer, I am in your midst (Matt. 18:20). Because I indwell you and all other saved people in your church, I want you to do exponential things for gospel outreach. Do you have obstacles? Are there mountains that stop you from going forward? Ask for faith to move mountains. You move problems first on your knees before you move them with your hands and head. Fast for God to remove obstacles, and pray for God to fill you with power for exponential outreach in evangelism. I am still alive, and the Holy Spirit is still available, ask for great spiritual breakthroughs in your church outreach: "According to your faith let it be to you" (Matt. 9:29, *NKJV*).

Lord, I want You to begin a revival in my heart. I need Your blessing and
power before I can touch the lives of others. Give me faith to believe You for
greater things and give me the boldness to witness for You. Fill me with the
Spirit and use me. Amen.

I am Jesus who grows churches (Eph. 4:16). Just as children grow when they have a proper diet and exercise, so to your church should be growing. Does it have a healthy diet of scripture teaching? Is it exercising evangelism to the lost? Everything in your Christian life begins in prayer, like the early church prayed and God increased their reach into the lost community. So let's pray, believe, work, and evangelize.

Lord, give me faith to obey the Great Commission.
Give me a burden to pray for lost people to get saved. Give me opportunities
to witness. Now give me boldness to do it. Amen.

READING: Hebrews 11:1-40

KEY THOUGHT: There must be great faith by leaders and people to solve problems and work to reach the community with the gospel.

I AM JESUS—*Exponential Praying*

"I will pour out My Spirit upon all people."

JOEL 2:29, NLT

"Suddenly, there was a sound from heaven like the roaring of a mighty windstorm . . . it filled the house . . . everyone was filled with the Holy Spirit."

ACTS 2:2, 4, NLT

I am Jesus who poured out the Holy Spirit on 120 believers on the Day of Pentecost. It didn't happen just because I promised to do it. It happened because they fasted and prayed and prepared to obey the Great Commission. They fasted and prayed for 50 days. That is a long time to continue praying and worshiping without seeing results. How long will you worship, and wait, and pray, to become an exponential church that will change the world? Remember, because they had the power of the Holy Spirit, it was said, "These that have turned the world upside down are come here also" (Acts 17:5, ELT). To get exponential results, you must be an exceptional follower. Go stand under the spigot, pray and wait for Me to fill you.

Lord, I want to change my world. I want to worship and pray exponentially. I want to testify and serve exponentially. I want to see exponential results in my church. Use me to begin. Amen.

I am Jesus who will make you an exceptional follower. If you let Me pour out the Holy Spirit on you, you can see exponential results in your prayer life, your Bible study, your ministry and your worship. Are you satisfied with the old life you lived before I came into your life? Begin by being filled with the Spirit. Stand, wait, pray, and believe.

Lord, I don't want a self-centered life like people in the world. I want to be Christ-centered. I want You to control my life. Control my thoughts . . . my desires . . . my work . . . and my leisure activities. I yield to You fully. Amen.

READING: Acts 12:5-19

KEY THOUGHT: When believers in a church seek the fullness of the Holy Spirit and let Him control their life and ministry, the church will have exponential blessings.

I AM JESUS—*Exponential Blessings*

"Those who believe . . . were baptized and added to the church . . . about 3000 in all."
ACTS 2:41, NLT

"All believers devoted themselves to . . . teaching . . . fellowship . . . sharing meals . . . prayer . . . worshiped together . . . and met in homes for the Lord's Supper."
ACTS 2:42, NLT

I am Jesus who poured exponential blessings on the new church. Those blessings were rapidly displayed in the church. They enjoyed My presence in their gatherings and they worshiped new and differently. They did not bring their animal sacrifices to the brazen altar. I was the Lamb slain to take away sins (John 1:29). They worshiped in their homes, and the streets belonged to the church to preach, testify, and serve. They went everywhere witnessing for Me. They experienced blessings never felt in the Old Testament. I had forgiven their sins, had indwelt their life, and had given them confidence and assurance never before realized. They were ministering directly for Me, not for the priest or temple. This was the age of the church—My presence in them. This was the age of the Holy Spirit—with exponential blessings.

Lord, I admit my faith is sometimes dull and uninspiring. I don't trust You for miracles, and I don't expect exponential blessings in my life. Forgive my sins, revive my spirit, and give me a new vision of how I can serve You and receive exponential blessings. Amen.

I am Jesus who gives exponential blessings to those who seek to do My perfect will for their life (Rom. 12:1). I will fill those with the Holy Spirit who seek and are yielded to Me (1 Cor. 3:16, Eph. 5:18). I will pour out exponential blessings on those who follow Me with exceptional faith.

Lord, I want more in my life than I now have. I want Your presence to fill me with joy so I can worship You with honesty. I want You to give me power in service so I can do exponential ministry for You. I wait for Your presence. Amen.

READING: Galatians 5:16-25

KEY THOUGHT: I will give exponential blessings to those who put Me first in their life and seek to serve Me with their entire life.

Day 7

I AM JESUS—*Less Than Exponential*

*"Write this letter to . . . the church in Laodicea . . . I know all the things you do,
that you are neither hot nor cold. I wish that you were one or the other!
But since you are like lukewarm water, neither hot nor cold,
I will spit you out of my mouth!"*

REV. 3:14-16, *NLT*

I am the church of all types of believers—some who have grown in their faith, others who are carnal, even babies in Christ (1 Cor. 3:1). Therefore, not all churches have a strong exponential outreach. Letters were written to the 7 churches (Rev. 2–3). One left its first love of evangelism (Rev. 2:5), another was ignorant of doctrine and fell into error (Rev. 2:12-17), and another had members living in sin and immorality (Rev. 2:18-20). There were other problems, so I challenged them, "repent and do the first works" (Rev. 2:5, *NKJV*). Actually the spiritually of churches is a reflection of the spirituality of its members. How spiritual is your church or its members? What must you do personally to have revival and become My exceptional followers?

Lord, sometimes I am blind to sin in my life (ignorant sin). Open my eyes to see anything that is holding me back. My problem is, I don't yield enough to You and I don't pursue godliness. Make me an exceptional follower so that my church will express exceptional evangelism and growth. Amen.

I indwell all believers, but not everyone is a shining testimony to the gospel light. Some have not tried to grow in their faith; others have given into temptation and sinned against Me. Sin blinds their spiritual eyes so they don't know what they do, nor do they know how blind they are to Me.

Lord, forgive my sin, cleanse me and make me usable. Fill me with the Holy Spirit to serve You effectively. Make me an exceptional follower. I want to be a member of an exponential church. Amen.

READING: Revelation 2:1-29

KEY THOUGHT: I want every follower to be an exceptional Christian, but they are not. I want every church to be an exponential church, but it isn't.

WEEK TWO

I AM JESUS:
A Church Revived

The key to exponential growth is revival strength from the Holy Spirit. God the Father promised, "I will pour out My Spirit." The pouring began at Pentecost and continues today. This week read how to begin a revival in your church and keep it going. The secret of a great exponential church is not with God but begins with you and your church. Revival is defined as "God pouring His presence on His people." To have the Holy Spirit poured on you, you must desire it, seek it, pray for it, and receive it when it comes. Don't you want the Father's presence? Don't you want revival? What is the secret? Go stand under the spout to find out.

Day 8

I AM JESUS—*A Church Revived*

"I will pour out My Spirit on all flesh."

JOEL 2:28, NLT

"Everyone was filled with the Holy Spirit."

ACTS 2:4, NLT

I am Jesus looking for My church to be revived. And what is revival? It is God pouring His presence on His people. That occurred on the Day of Pentecost, and I can revive your church. To get revived, you and the other members of your church must wait in prayer. What do you think they were doing as they waited for Pentecost? How do you think they prayed? They confessed and begged for My presence, they interceded for their lost friends and family, they worshiped, they fasted! Wrapped up in their intercession was sacrifice. It takes sacrifice to get the full blessings of God. You must empty out self and fill your life with My presence.

Lord, I need revival. Motivate my heart to seek revival. I have hidden sin there (ignorant sin); cleanse me and point me to Your cross. Help me sacrifice as You did on the cross. Send revival to my church and do it through me. Amen.

I am Jesus, wanting to revive your church. Yes, I want to give you joy and blessings, but most of all, I want to evangelize lost people in your neighborhood. I want you to go get them saved, then baptize them and put them into ministry, helping you do the work of evangelism. I want My house filled.

Lord, forgive me for only looking at my needs and my problems. Give me eyes to see Your church and help me revive it. Use me in evangelism to reach the lost around me. Amen.

READING: Luke 14:16-35

KEY THOUGHT: Churches that are not exponential in outreach need to be revived. I need to pour the Holy Spirit on them.

I AM JESUS—A *Spirit-filled Church*

*"Don't be drunk with wine, because that will ruin your life.
Instead, be filled with the Holy Spirit."*

EPH. 5:18, NLT

You as a believer can be filled with the Holy Spirit. When you and others in your church are filled with the Spirit, you become an awesome tool. When Paul and Barnabas took the gospel to Antioch in Turkey, many were saved in the Jewish synagogue (Acts 12:14-52). The unbelieving Jews attacked the new Gentile believers because they were filled with envy (13:45). But "the word of the Lord was published throughout the region because the believers were filled with joy and with the Holy Spirit" (Acts 13:49, ELT). When they were filled with the Holy Spirit, exponential aggressive evangelism resulted. Perhaps you or your church have not experienced evangelism because you are not Holy Spirit filled (Luke 14:23).

Lord, I am empty; fill me with the Holy Spirit. I am not accomplishing much for Your kingdom; fill me with the Holy Spirit. I want to be an effective witness for You and I want my church to grow. Amen.

To be filled with the Holy Spirit first you must empty yourself of sin and pride. I won't fill dirty vessels. Next, you must ask the Holy Spirit to fill your thoughts, desires and relationships. I won't go where I am not welcome. The third step is filling your life with the Word of God. The Bible will control your thoughts, desires and actions. The filling of the Holy Spirit and scriptures go hand in hand. You won't get one without the other. So, the first step begins with you.

Lord, I want to be used in aggressive evangelism—fill me with the Spirit. I will read, memorize and meditate on Your Word; let it control my life. I ask You now, start filling me with the Holy Spirit, and don't stop till I am filled up to the brim. Amen.

READING: Acts 13:14-52

KEY THOUGHT: The Holy Spirit is available and wants to fill you, but it begins with your wanting Him and asking Him to fill you.

I AM JESUS—*Sender of the Holy Spirit*

"I will ask the Father and He will give you . . . the Holy Spirit, who leads into all truth."
JOHN 14:16, *NLT*

I will send the Holy Spirit to do many things for you. He will convict (cause to see) your sin (John 16:8). He will show you biblical truth (John 14:26). He will fill you with authority to do ministry (Eph. 5:18). He will give you authority in ministry so that lost people are saved and believers grow. He will guide you in daily living (Gal. 5:18). He will build Christian character in your life, called the fruit of the Spirit (Gal. 5:22-23). He has energy to motivate you to repentance, to deeper prayers, and to exponential evangelism. Don't try to serve the heavenly Father on your own or out of habit. Ask the Holy Spirit to fill you and use you.

Lord, I need a fresh touch from Your presence. Lately I haven't been productive in Your ministry. Fill me with the Holy Spirit. I yield to You and seek Your power in my life. Amen.

The Holy Spirit won't come to exalt Himself (John 16:13). He will quietly exalt Me in your life (Phil. 1:27) and will lead you in "Spirit worship" of the Father (John 4:23-24). He will give you authority and power in ministry (Acts 1:8). Don't you need the Holy Spirit today to help you succeed in your ministry and Christian living? If your life has fallen into a daily routine, ask the Holy Spirit to fill you and use you.

Holy Spirit, come revive my vision of serving and living for the Father. Come revive my ministry for Jesus. Come, Holy Spirit, give me inner joy and confidence in all I do for You. Amen.

READING: John 4:21-25; 14:15-26

KEY THOUGHT: When your Christian life becomes ordinary and habitual, you need the presence of the Holy Spirit to revive and use you.

I AM JESUS—*A Spirit-motivated Church*

"God revealed these things by his Spirit.
For his Spirit searches out everything and shows us God's deep secrets."

I COR. 2:10, *NLT*

I am Jesus who will send the Holy Spirit into your life and into your church. When you yield to the Holy Spirit and let Him control your life—and the life of your church—you will live and serve in a new experience of happiness and effectiveness. This book is about you being an exceptional follower of Me, so the first step is to ask the Holy Spirit to fill you (Eph. 5:18) and direct your daily life and service (Gal. 5:16, 25). Are you tired of striving for the things of outward satisfaction? Tired of trying to make a name for yourself and struggling to get ahead? Invite the Holy Spirit to control your life. Follow His lead and ask Him for power to do spiritual things you cannot do (Phil. 4:13).

Holy Spirit, come into my life to convict me of any ignorant sin (John 16:8).
Forgive me and cleanse all sin (1 John 1:9). Fill me with Your presence and lead
me today. Amen.

When the Holy Spirit comes into your life, He not only will show you where you have gone wrong, He will show you the Father's plan for your life: "I know the plans I have for you . . . they are plans for good and not for disaster, to give you a future and a hope" (Jer. 29:11, *NLT*). Why don't you pray for the Father's plans right now; they may have been a secret to you, but the Holy Spirit will reveal them to you.

Holy Spirit, I fall into a routine of earning money and taking care of business.
I yield to You. Come reveal Your plans for my life. I am excited about
my future. Amen.

READING: 1 Corinthians 2:1-15

KEY THOUGHT: The Holy Spirit has a plan for your life. Take the initiative to find it and do it.

I AM JESUS—*In Revival*

"Then if my people who are called by my name will humble themselves
and pray and seek my face and turn from their wicked ways,
I will hear from heaven and will forgive their sins and restore their land."

2 CHRONICLES. 7:14, *NLT*

My people will have revival when they follow the formula in today's verse. First, they must humble themselves by admitting their selfish and egotistical desires by yielding everything to Me. Next, they must pray just as the first church prayed for 10 days between My ascension to heaven and Pentecost. The third step for revival is to seek My face. Remember, revival is described as pouring out My presence on My people. When the Shekinah glory cloud fell on the tabernacle, the people were revived. The fourth step is turning from your wicked ways. Quit all those activities that I disapprove of and repent of all known sin. That formula worked in the Old Testament and has worked in the church for 2,000 years. Are you ready for My presence to revive you and your church?

Lord, I admit I am selfish and seek my pride rather than Your glory. I cannot revive myself; I am too sinful. Send the Holy Spirit to revive me by visiting me daily and using me in service. Come, Holy Spirit, fill and revive me. Amen.

Your heart is the secret of revival. The Holy Spirit is always ready to come fill My church and energize My people. The heavenly Father seeks worship (John 4:27, 28), and I want to be preeminent in your life and church (Col. 1:18). We want you to be revived; it is the way you will live in heaven; it will be an added blessing and happiness to your life on Earth. Make a decision to start now to seek the Holy Spirit's presence in revival.

Lord, I simply ask You to revive me. I will obey You, follow You, and serve You. Fill me and use me. Amen.

READING: Colossian 1:15-20; Joel 2:12-32

KEY THOUGHT: The key to revival is found in 2 Chronicles 7:14, and you can determine the period when the Holy Spirit will come.

I AM JESUS—Keeping Revival

"So I say let the Holy Spirit guide your lives."
COLOSSIANS 5:16, *NLT*

"Since we are living by the Spirit, let us follow the Spirit's leading in every part of our lives."
GALATIANS 5:25, *NLT*

What happens when revival comes? You cannot just sit back to enjoy His presence. You must do something to keep revival going. When the Holy Spirit manifests His presence, keep living daily and do those things that brought revival. Follow His leading, go where He leads you, and do what He tells you to do. You have the Holy Spirit; now let Him work through you to testify to lost people and other believers who need revival. Do the work of ministry and let the Holy Spirit work through you. If you don't work with the Holy Spirit and allow Him to work through you, you will lose revival. The Spirit comes to work mightily in your church. If you cannot do what He has come to do, you will block out revival.

Holy Spirit, I want revival and ask You to pour Your presence on me and my church. I will let You lead me when You come, and I will minister with You. Send revival to my soul; I need it. Amen.

To keep revival in your life and church, you must continue doing those spiritual disciplines that brought revival in the first place. Don't grieve the Holy Spirit (Eph. 4:30), which is doing sinful things in your life. Also, don't quench the Holy Spirit (1 Thess. 5:19). When you snuff out a light, you quench its illumination. So don't do anything that is contrary to the holy nature of the Spirit. Don't snuff out His light.

Holy Spirit, come revive me and my church. I will not do anything to grieve You, nor will I put out the light of Your testimony in my life. I will pray as hard to keep revival as I did to originally get it. Amen.

READING: Acts 5:1-11; Eph. 4:20-32

KEY THOUGHT: When the Holy Spirit comes in revival, let Him guide you in your actions and life.

I AM JESUS— *Reviving Ministry*

"There are different kinds of spiritual gifts, but the same Spirit is the source of them all. There are different kinds of service . . . same Lord. God works in different ways, but it is the same God who does the work in all of us."

1 CORINTHIANS. 12:4-6, NLT

When the Holy Spirit is poured out on you in revival, it is not just for enjoyment. The Spirit comes into the church to enhance the ministry of each person in the church. He gives different spiritual gifts (abilities) to each believer. But He is the same Spirit working in each person but ministering differently. That is the beauty of one body: all the members work together for the same goal of carrying out the Great Commission. So to keep revival going, keep doing what you did to get revival. But remember, the Holy Spirit revives His church to carry out ministry for the Father. What are you and your church doing to keep revival fires burning?

Holy Spirit, You have given me spiritual gifts. I will use them to glorify the Father. I will work in harmony with You to keep revival going. Thank You for opportunities, and thank You for challenges. I will not give up. Amen.

Find the proper spiritual gift for you to use in ministry. First look in the rear-view mirror where you have been successful (Josh. 1:8), that might suggest where you should minister in the future. Listen to your friends and fellow workers; sometimes their counsel will help you know where to minister best (Prov. 10:14). Also, pray for the Holy Spirit to guide you into the most effective ministry for your spiritual gift. Finally, remember the principle of open doors. Opportunities may be the most effective place for your ministry.

Holy Spirit, I yield to You. Fill me for ministry. Guide me to ministry. Then use me in ministry. Amen.

READING: 1 Corinthians 12:1-31

KEY THOUGHT: When revival comes, the Holy Spirit is opening new doors of ministry. Find the best opportunity for your ministry and do it.

WEEK THREE

I AM JESUS
A Church Witnessing

Last week you read about the power of the Holy Spirit when He is poured out on a church. This week you will focus on using His power to witness to the world. You must first witness to them your salvation from sin and your transformation by the power of Jesus Christ. Then you must go in the power of the Holy Spirit to share the message with family, friends and the neighborhood. Finally, you will read how your church can plant churches around the world.

I AM JESUS—*A Witnessing Church*

"We cannot stop telling about everything we have seen and heard."

ACTS 4:20, *NLT*

I am Jesus, challenging you to witness to everyone about your salvation and love for Me. When I was on Earth, it was natural for Me to share My life and mission with everyone I touched. Now I live in you, so I want to speak through you to all you meet. Tell them of forgiveness of your sins and that I have a special place for your life (Jer. 2:9-11). But more than that, you are part of a New Testament church. I challenged My disciples to be My witnesses beginning at their house in Jerusalem and extending to Judea, which was the surrounding area. So you should join with your church to be My witnesses in your home area and outlying communities.

Lord, forgive me when I have been bashful and afraid to witness for You to my friends and family. Give me courage to share my testimony with others and give me wisdom to do it effectively. Amen.

I am Jesus, the power behind your testimony. I am the One who forgave all your sins when you called on Me for salvation. Now, I am the One living in your heart (Gal. 2:2). Let My presence in your life strengthen you to speak. Remember, those first disciples said, "We cannot stop telling about everything we have seen and heard" (Acts 4:20, *NLT*). Just share the Good News that changed your life, and it will change the lives of others.

Lord, thank You for the privilege of being a witness for You. I don't deserve this privilege, and I am not that good of a testimony, but I will tell my friends and fellow workers what You have done for me. Use me. Amen.

READING: Acts 1:1-9; 4:1-20

KEY THOUGHT: A witness is one who testifies to others what Jesus has done for them and how He has changed their life.

I AM JESUS—*A Church Growing*

"For we are both God's workers. And you are God's field."

1 CORINTHIANS. 3:9, *NLT*

"Yes, I am the vine; you are the branches. Those who remain in me,
and I in them, will produce much fruit. For apart from me you can do nothing."

JOHN 15:5, *NLT*

I am Jesus the Church. In Scripture My church is pictured as a garden, or a planted field, or a farm. It is a place where living seeds are planted to grow into food to eat or flowers for beauty. I produce eternal life when the seed of Scripture is planted in human hearts. In your church you see various believers in different stages of growth. Some are like newly planted seeds with growth potential. Some believers have new fruit; others have ripened fruit. But then others need pruning to get rid of dead branches that will kill, or fungus that will stunt growth: "I am the vine; you are the branches. Those who remain in me, and I in them, will produce much fruit" (John 15:5, *NLT*).

Lord, I want to be a healthy growing plant in Your garden. I need the water of the Word of God to grow, and the sunshine of answered prayer. I need cultivation around the roots to get life-giving air into my system. Lord, prune me where I need it. Amen.

I am the Church where you grow and bear fruit. I have life-giving energy to produce life through you. The secret to fruitfulness is your relationship with Me. Let My life flow into you to receive all the nutrients you need. I want to flow into you and through you. Growing a garden never ends; even after harvest in the fall, the field must be prepared for the next crop, next year. Your life is a garden that is life-growing.

Lord, it's a privilege to grow in Your garden. Produce life through me that is beautiful and nutritious. I want to accomplish everything in life that You have chosen for me to be and do. Amen.

READING: John 15:1-7

KEY THOUGHT: The church is pictured as a farm, or field, or garden that is planted, cultivated, and harvested to feed others.

I AM JESUS—*A Church Sharing the Good News*

"'We gave you strict orders never again to teach in this man's name!' he said. 'Instead, you have filled all Jerusalem with your teaching about him.'"

ACTS 5:28, NLT

The disciples went all over Jerusalem telling everyone about Me, Jesus. Their bold testimony got them in trouble with the authorities. They told their accusers, "We must obey God rather than any human authority" (v. 29). That is what I want you to do: tell everyone the Good News that I died to forgive their sins. Give them a testimony of My power that has changed your life. After all, I am more important to you than anything else (Phil. 1:21), and I can do more for them than anyone else. I need you to tell them the Good News. I can't do it; I am in heaven. Let Me minister to your friends and family through your testimony and acts of kindness. After all, you may be the only gospel testimony they ever experience.

Lord, I sometimes forget to share salvation with them. Forgive me. Fill me with the power that You promised (Acts 1:8), and I will tell them that my sins are forgiven, that I have been redeemed, and that I serve You. Amen.

The disciples filled Jerusalem teaching everyone about Me. They used every opportunity to share the gospel with everyone who would listen to them, and they did it at every available occasion and time. Now you should think of creative ways to tell friends and family about Me. The more often they hear about Me, the more likely they will be converted.

Lord, show me creative ways to share my testimony with friends and family. Help me use every opportunity to give my testimony of how I got saved. Help me to reach every friend and relative with the gospel. Help me use time wisely when I am with them to share the power of Your saving grace in my life. Amen.

READING: Acts 5:17-42

KEY THOUGHT: The early church didn't limit their ministry to announced church times but used every available occasion and every available method to reach every available person with the gospel.

I AM JESUS—A Church Reaching Lost People

"How I kept back nothing that was helpful, but proclaimed it to you,
and taught you publicly and from house to house, testifying to Jews, and also to Greeks,
repentance toward God and faith toward our Lord Jesus Christ."

ACTS 20:20-22, NKJV

Paul shared the gospel in public gatherings and went house to house to try to win people to salvation. He was doing more than distributing Christian literature or inviting people to attend church. He was sharing the gospel by "testifying to Jews, and also to Greeks, repentance toward God and faith toward our Lord Jesus Christ" (v. 21). Paul did what some modern-day churches forget—he evangelized. I am Jesus who gave the Great Commission to My followers to preach "into all the world . . . to every creature" (Mark 16:15, *NKJV*). In Matthew 28:19 (*NKJV*), I also said, "Make disciples of all the nations (tribes)." Therefore, evangelize every person, in every part of the world, and disciple new believers of all people groups. Is your church obeying Me?

Lord, forgive me when I had a hard heart or was unresponsive to Your
Commission. Burden my heart to pray for lost people and may I attempt to reach
them with the gospel. May I win at least one person to salvation. Amen.

I am Jesus who commanded you to evangelize all. You could do it several ways. You could do personal evangelism, i.e., one on one. Or you could get involved in your church's evangelistic outreach. Then there are other para-church organizations that are reaching lost people. You could minister with them in other ways to fully support foreign missions with your time, talent and offerings. If today believers were as evangelistic as the first-century church in evangelism, the Great Commission could be finished.

Lord, I pray for churches everywhere to work hard to fulfill the
Great Commission. Forgive our failures and give us spiritual power to
reach them all. Amen.

READING: Acts 20:13-38

KEY THOUGHT: When Jesus gave the Great Commission, He expected His followers to be both enthusiastic and energetic in spreading it to all people.

29

I AM JESUS—A Body Exercising

*"Their responsibility is to equip God's people to do his work a
nd build up the church, the body of Christ."*

EPHESIANS 4:12, *NLT*

I am Jesus, the Church body. Did you see today's verse that said, "Build up the church"? How do you build up a body? Exercise! Not once but by doing it many times. To build up My Church body, you need to win souls. Not once but many times. But exercise cannot be a little effort, not to build a physical body. You must exercise till you sweat, till you are exhausted. Have you tried to win lost people with all your heart and energy? Have you continued trying to win souls till you were exhausted? The gym instructor tells you; "no pain, no gain." So I challenge you "no total effor, no church growth." One more thing about exercise: it gets harder each day, more intense each day, more difficult each day. Have you gotten to the place where it is difficult to win people to Me? If so, then you are just beginning. Keep up the hard work, the smart work, the rewarding work.

Lord, I want my church body to grow. Sometimes time I see no growth; at other times I see little growth. But I will not stop. I will keep exercising till I see measurable growth, consistent growth. Amen.

I am Jesus, your Church body. Don't think of Me as an organization, or budget, or program. I am working on you to build up My church. I am the Church body reaching out to capture lost people to incorporate them into My body. I cannot do it without you, and you cannot do it without Me. We are church! Let's get lost people into our body.

Lord, when I am not effective, show me how to serve You. When I have little fruit, make me more effective. When I am discouraged, speak to me, motivate me, fill me. Then send me out to serve You. Amen.

READING: Ephesians 4:1-16

KEY THOUGHT: Just as a physical body is built with exercise, so too the spiritual church body is built by spiritual exercise.

I AM JESUS—Adding to My Church

"Those who believed what Peter said were baptized and added to the church that day—about 3,000 in all. All the believers devoted themselves to the apostles' teaching, and to fellowship, and to sharing in meals (including the Lord's Supper), and to prayer."

ACTS 2:41-42, NLT

I am Jesus, the Church body of Christ left on the earth when I was resurrected to ascend to heaven. There were 120 praying in the Upper Room (Acts 1:15). After Peter preached a powerful sermon on Pentecost, "Those who believed . . . were baptized and added to the church" (Acts 1:41, *NLT*). A few weeks later Peter preached again: "The number of believers now totaled about 5,000" (Acts 4:4, *NLT*). These were the heads of families, so about 20,000 were in the church. Next, "believers rapidly multiplied" (Acts 6:1, *NLT*). Then believers grew exponentially: "Believers greatly increased" (Acts 6:7, NLT). Finally, it was no longer the growth of believers, "The churches . . . were multiplied" (Acts 9:31, *NKJV*). When the number of churches grew exponentially, that explosion was super-aggressive growth. Pray for that increase in your church.

Lord, thank You for my salvation and for those who have found salvation in my church. I want to see exponential growth in my church: "Increase our faith" (Luke 17:5, NKJV). You are the God who caused the first church to grow; do it again. Amen.

But the church in Jerusalem had more than numbers. It was growing internally and spiritually. They were learning the Word daily (Acts 1:42, 5:42). They continued praying (Acts 1:42, 5:31), they gave sacrificially (Acts 1:44, 11:29), and God gave them exponential blessings (Acts 1:42-47). Because they followed Me fully, they became exceptional Christians who built an exponential church. If you and all the others in your church grew mightily, so would your church.

Lord, I pray to be an exceptional believer so that my church will grow exponentially. Amen.

READING: Acts 2:1-13, 42-47; 4:1-4

KEY THOUGHT: The early church had exponential growth because the believers were exceptional followers of Jesus.

I AM JESUS—*Continuous Witnessing*

"The high priest confronted them (the church) . . .
you have filled all Jerusalem with your teaching."

ACTS 5:28, NLT

"And every day, in the temple and from house to house,
they continued to preach and teach . . . Jesus is Messiah."

ACTS 5:42, NLT

I am a church that continually witnesses the message of salvation. I tell every person from young to old, from rich to poor, and from Jew to Gentile. But more than that, I want to witness all the time in every place. Why do My followers witness continuously? Because I said, "I am the way . . . no one can come to the Father except through Me" (John 14:6, *NLT*). I am the only One who can save all people. And I love all people (John 3:16). So witness to them My love. Not only that, invite them into My body—the church—the greatest privilege in the world, with the greatest benefits and blessings. Since you are My followers, you must witness about Me to all.

Lord, thank You for saving me and transforming me with the gospel
message. Forgive me for not witnessing to others. Give me an inner
compulsion to witness to my lost friends and family. Amen.

My command is one more reason to witness to all people, at all times, using all methods: "You shall be witnesses to Me" (Acts 1:8, *NKJV*). When you become a Christian, the Holy Spirit comes into your life. Now let Him use you to witness about Me in your home area to win your Jerusalem. Then witness in the surrounding areas, next the "large" state or provinces, and finally use all your witnessing influence to change the world.

Lord, I will obey and begin witnessing to family and friends today. Amen.

READING: Acts 5:29-42; 11:19-21

KEY THOUGHT: It is imperative for every follower to witness to everyone they know to reach and change the world.

WEEK FOUR

I AM JESUS:
A Teaching Church

When you evangelize new converts that come to salvation, then you must obey the second part of the Great Commission, i.e., "Teaching them to obey all things I taught you" (Matt. 28:20, ELT). Super-aggressive evangelism must lead to exponential teaching. The new converts must be taught about Me and what I can do for them. Teaching begins at the earliest age and extends to the senior citizen members. The ministry of teaching includes the new converts receiving salvation and extends to the more mature believers in the church. It includes teaching Bible content, Christian living, attitudes, and all other matter. What happens when a church obeys the teaching mandate? "I am with you to the ends of the earth" (Matt. 28:20, ELT).

Day 22

I AM JESUS—*Exponential Teaching*

"Daily in the temple and house to house, they ceased not to teach and preach."

ACTS 5:42, KJV

"The church leaders said, 'We will give ourselves continually to prayer and to the ministry of the Word.'"

ACTS 6:4, KJV

I am the early church that continually gave itself to the Word of God. The leaders gave themselves to teaching, and new converts gave themselves to learning. The new church was grounded on Scripture and teaching. As a result, individuals followed Me. And that is why the Christian experienced exponential growth. My Word is alive (John 6:63), and it is powerful (Heb. 4:12). When you properly teach the Word of God, you are preparing for explosive growth. Why? Because super-aggressive teaching of Scripture leads to exponential growth

Lord, I want my church to experience exponential growth. I will learn the Word of God for myself, and I will teach it super-aggressively. Then, Lord, I ask You to grow the church and change the world. Amen.

I am Jesus, who will bless the church with exponential growth when the foundation is laid with solid Bible teaching. Then you must follow with aggressive faith, aggressive witnessing, and aggressive outreach of the gospel. Do you want to change the world? There is a predetermined formula that works.

Lord, I pray for my church to change the world. But first, Lord, change me. Make me a super-aggressive witness. Then, Lord, help me motivate people in my church to a greater vision. Then, Lord, help us change our world. Then perhaps we can change the rest of the world. Amen.

READING: Acts 2:42-46; 4:4-24; 8:4-8

KEY THOUGHT: The gospel is the only message that saves people from hell, and the Great Commission is the only method to preach the gospel to everyone to change the world.

Day 23

I AM JESUS—*Teaching New Followers*

"Teach these new disciples to obey all the commands I have given you."

MATTHEW 28:20, *NLT*

"Those . . . added to the church . . . devoted themselves to the apostle's teaching."

ACTS 2:41-42, *NLT*

I am Jesus, teaching new believers. Did you see two things in today's verses? First, I commanded the church to teach new disciples all My commands. Second, the church got people saved and then they taught them. Early exponential church growth was based on teaching new converts My commands. Is your church doing that today? When hundreds in a neighborhood become new followers, teach them what to believe and train them how to live for Me. Do that and you will change a neighborhood. How can you change the world? Get people saved, then teach them what to believe and how to live for Me. Then reproduce that result in another new church.

Lord, forgive me for not studying Your Word more and knowing You better. Help me learn great truths about You I don't know. Send the Holy Spirit to teach me (John 14:16) and help me remember (John 14:26). Help me to be a learning, growing, useful follower of Yours. Amen.

I am the Church, and in Me all types of teaching go on. Babies are being taught; older people are being taught. People are being taught how to serve, how to lead, and how to be better parents and examples to lost people. All kinds of people are teaching: church leaders, older women teaching younger women, parents teaching their children. And teaching is going on in Sunday school classes, for all ages, and all needs, and all different subjects. I want My church to be a teaching church.

Lord, thank You for my parents, who taught me many things. I will teach my family and children. Thank You for all types of teachers in my church. Help me learn, grow, and serve You better. I will teach. Amen.

READING: Matthew 13:1-23

KEY THOUGHT: Scripture is filled with commands and illustrations of teaching. You can't build a church on teaching; you build it on evangelism. You can't build a church without teaching.

I AM JESUS—*A Teaching Church*

"But the comforter, the Holy Spirit . . . He will teach you all things."
JOHN 14:26, NLT

"When He, the Spirit of truth, is come, He will guide you into all truth."
JOHN 16:13, NLT

The One who guides your understanding in My church is the Holy Spirit. Did you see one of His names is *Spirit of Truth?* He will guide you into truth. Guiding is what a teacher does: "Teaching is the guidance of learning activities." Teaching is not just telling a lesson. No! A teacher guides the learning activities; it is learning that changes the life of the student. The teacher hasn't taught until the student has learned the intended lesson. It is the Holy Spirit in the heart of the teacher Who guides the learning process.

Lord, thank You for all I have learned. I don't know all. I want to learn even more of Your Word and more about You. I want to teach others what I am learning; give me a classroom of one or many. Use me to teach. Amen.

When Philip witnessed to the Ethiopian eunuch in his chariot, he asked, "Do you understand what you read?" He was reading the book of Isaiah. The Ethiopian official answered, "How can I, unless someone instructs me?" (Acts 8:31, NKJV). Did you see that word *guide?* Both the Holy Spirit and human teachers are needed to guide people to understand the Word of God.

Holy Spirit, I cannot teach, but You can do it through me. I cannot change the life of another; but Holy Spirit, You can do it through me. Come, Holy Spirit, fill my life. Use my teaching. I want to change the life of another to be like Jesus. Amen.

READING: John 14:16-26; Acts 8:26-39

KEY THOUGHT: Great teachers guide the learning experience of students, but the Holy Spirit must guide both teacher and student.

I AM JESUS—*Prepare and Teach*

"Study to shew thyself approved unto God, a workman that needeth not to be ashamed, rightly dividing the word of truth."

2 TIMOTHY 2:15, *NLT*

"Continue in the things you have learned."

2 TIMOTHY 3:14, *NLT*

"Meditate on these things."

1 TIMOTHY 4:15, *NLT*

I am a church with human teachers and learners. Before you can teach, you must learn the lessons you would teach. The church is primarily a place of evangelism, and second, a place of education. Those who know the most Christian doctrine should teach the most. Those who know best how to live for Christ teach best. And those who know Christ intimately teach and change lives of others. What do you know most and best about your Christian faith? How much of it have you taught? Those who know best teach others who have learned.

Lord, forgive me for being lazy and not learning more about my faith and knowing You better. Teach me those things I don't know. Show me where I am ignorant, so I can learn and grow and have intimate fellowship with You (Phil. 3:10-14). Amen.

I am a church on a teaching mission. You will never know it all, and you will never know enough. You were born in this world with a blank slate mind. How much you learn will determine how much you will grow. And how practically you learn the Christian life will determine how effective you will live for Me.

Lord, I will read Your Word, repeatedly. I will study Your Word, dividing truth into small sections to learn. I will memorize Your Word, hiding it in my heart (Ps. 119:11). Then I will meditate on Your Word, so its life principles control my life (Josh. 1:8; Ps. 1:5). Amen.

READING: Joshua 1:6-9; Psalms 1:1-6; 119:9-16

KEY THOUGHT: My church shall be a place of teaching-learning, because neither are effective until both are operative.

Day 26

I AM JESUS—A Reproducing Church

"You have heard me teach things that have been confirmed by many reliable witnesses. Now teach these truths to other trustworthy people who will be able to pass them on to others."

2 TIMOTHY. 2:2, *NLT*

I am a church that will die if the children and new converts are not taught church belief and the practices I taught you. In today's scripture, Paul taught young Timothy the principle of reproduction. Paul was the first generation passing Christianity on to the second generation. But it doesn't stop there. Timothy must then teach everything he learned to the third generation, called "trustworthy people." This means they were worthy of the trust Timothy had in them. Then the third generation must teach the fourth generation. They are called "others." What Paul taught was not properly learned until it influenced the third generation. How do we know Timothy did as good a job as Paul? Because the third generation passed the lesson on to the fourth generation. Is your church teaching its children, grand-children, and great-grandchildren?

Lord, I have failed in many ways. But I don't want to fail as a teacher. Help me teach Your doctrine and the Christian life to my children then my grandchildren and ultimately my great-grandchildren. Amen.

Let's see how this works. I taught Andrew in his first day of ministry (John 1:38-40). Then Andrew brought his brother Peter (second generation) to be a follower of Mine (John 1:41-42). Then Peter preached on Pentecost and over 300 got saved. They could be described as the third spiritual generation. Then, they went back to their homes and spread the gospel, i.e., a fourth generation of Jesus followers.

Lord, I want fruit in my life. May I help someone to salvation. Then may I teach them what to believe and how to live, so they can go to teach someone else. Lord, multiply my life. Amen.

READING: John 1:35-42; Acts 2:5-12, 41-47

KEY THOUGHT: The secret to successful teaching is when your students can share what they have learned with someone else and then they pass it on.

Day 27

I AM JESUS—*A Teaching Church for the Young*

"And you must commit yourselves wholeheartedly to these commands . . . repeat them again and again to your children . . . when you are at home . . . on the road . . . going to bed and . . . getting up."

DEUTERONOMY 6:6-7, *NLT*

"Timothy . . . your genuine faith . . . first filled your grandmother Lois, and your mother Eunice."

2 TIMOTHY 1:5, *NLT*

I want My church diligently teaching all children. Timothy was an early church leader who was first taught by his grandmother, then his mother. Paul reminded him, "You have been taught the holy scriptures from childhood" (2 Tim. 3:15, *NLT*). That is the example for all churches today. When this standard is reached, then growing exponential churches can change the world by producing reproducing believers. Satan wants to capture everyone in My church, and he will start with those most vulnerable—the children. Protect your children; teach them about Me. Guarantee your church's future; teach the children.

Lord, forgive me where I have been slack teaching children. They are so young and have great futures before them. Help me reach children with salvation, and then teach them the Scriptures. I want a strong leader like Timothy to come out of my church. So I will pray and teach. Amen.

A child is born with a blank slate. They must learn to talk, walk and feed themselves. They must be taught to read, write and communicate. Make sure they learn basic Christianity, how to follow Me. Then they must learn basic beliefs, knowledge about God, sin, salvation and Christian service. The more they learn, the stronger Christians they will become. The better they are trained, the more they can do for Me and the church. I love churches that teach the young.

Lord, it's clear You have commanded us to teach the children. Forgive me and forgive my church where we have failed. I want to teach children and I want my children to be strong future leaders for You. Amen.

READING: Deuteronomy 6:1-9; Mark 10:13-16; Acts 16:1-5

KEY THOUGHT: Everything you know about Christianity will be lost to the church when you die, so teach the young so that they can replace you and they can teach the next generation.

39

Day 28

I AM JESUS—*Teaching Scriptures*

"But you must remain faithful to the things you have been taught . . . the holy Scriptures from childhood, and they have given you the wisdom to receive the salvation . . . all Scripture is inspired by God and is useful to teach us what is true and to make us realize what is wrong in our lives."

2 TIMOTHY 3:14-16, *NLT*

The church teaches Scriptures not just to know it or be smart but to lead you to salvation. Timothy was saved because the Bible had been taught to him as a child. The Bible is the most important lesson for a child to learn in church. The Bible will convict you of wrong doing (2 Tim. 3:16), so you will get saved. The Bible has My life in it (John 6:63); it will give you eternal life. The Bible will help you find a plan and purpose for your life. The Bible will give you assurances of salvation (1 John 5:13) and take away doubt and fear. The Bible will help you find My presence in prayer. Don't you need to ask Me something (John 15:7)?

Lord, I will study Your Scriptures for confidence and direction. Guide me with Your Word (Ps. 119:105). I want to hide Your Word in my heart to keep from sinning against You (Ps. 119:11). Amen.

I am the Word of God incarnate (John 1:1, 14). I teach My Word in My church to transform sinners into children of God and to make babes in Christ grow to maturity (Heb. 5:11-14). I teach My Word that grows workmen into powerful pulpit preachers. My Word will make silly girls into godly women intercessors. Let's teach My Word.

Lord, help me take every opportunity to teach Your Word. Help me to teach all people—new believers and wise people— Your Word. I love Your Word; it has changed my life. Use me to teach others to also change them. Amen.

READING: 2 Timothy 3:10-17; John 1:1-18

KEY THOUGHT: Teach the Bible to produce many different changes in people, in many different types of people.

WEEK FIVE

I AM JESUS
A Ministering and Serving Church

This fifth week focuses on the ways you can minister in your church. Everyone has a spiritual gift or ability to serve the Father. That ability gives them an obligation to minister with all their heart for the glory of the Father. Also, it will lead to the exponential expansion of the church. The secret of a growing church is when all members minister and serve sacrificially to carry out the Great Commission. When that is done, the church will continue growing exponentially to bring glory to God the Father.

Day 29

I AM JESUS—*A Church Ministering*

"A great famine . . . so the believers in Antioch decided to send relief . . . everyone giving as much as they could."
ACTS 11:28-29, NLT

When a church is ministering to the poor, needy and helpless, that is Me showing My love through My church. It may be the hands of men and women in the church, but it is My hands. My church should never allow people to starve; it should give to demonstrate My love. Then they will listen to the gospel that will save them. You must think both physical and spiritual needs. You cannot minister one without the other. Look at My example while on Earth. I ministered to people whether or not they were My followers. And many began following Me because of "love in action."

Lord, I confess to being stingy sometimes. Forgive me. Help me look at people through Your eyes. Help me look beyond a physical problem into their heart. Then help me to communicate Your gospel to people. Healing the physical body is love in action, but healing a lost soul is eternal. Amen.

No church can do all things to help all people at all times. But begin at home; minister to those in your family then those in your neighborhood. But remember, it is not giving money, or food, or physical healing. It is about your relationship to Me. Let My compassion flow through you. Then it is about your relationship to your family and church. You cannot neglect them. Then look beyond your church limits; look for avenues to help, heal, and offer eternal salvation.

Lord, I want to minister for You. Show me how, where, and when. Here am I, use me. Amen.

READING: Acts 11:19-30; 6:1-7

KEY THOUGHT: All humans ought to be compassionate and helpful to those around them, but the followers of Jesus must give first, give most, and give the gospel.

I AM JESUS—*A Church of Ministers*

"Determined to send relief . . . by the hands of Barnabas and Saul."
ACTS 11:29-30, *NLT*

"But the word of God grew and multiplied . . . they returned . . .
when they had fulfilled their ministry."
ACTS 12:24-25, *NLT*

My church prospers when ministry is properly done. In today's verses, the church at Antioch sent money and supplies to Jerusalem because of a famine. But the money didn't just feed hungry people. There was spiritual ministry with their money: "The word of God grew and multiplied" (Acts 12:24, *NKJV*). That means two things. First, the influence of Scripture spread over the area. Next, people responded to the God of the Bible by preaching of those who fed them; some were saved, and the church grew. Second, it meant the church was growing in understanding and use of the Word.

Lord, thank You for the opportunity of ministering both to the physical and spiritual needs of others. I will not do one without the other; I will do both at the same time. Give me a heart for needy people, both physical and spiritual. Amen.

In today's passage, Barnabas and Saul left Antioch to travel a long distance to minister to the physical needs of Jerusalem. That is the city that crucified Me and persecuted My church. Why go there? Remember I said, "Repay no one evil for evil . . . if your enemy is hungry feed him" (Rom. 12:17, 20, *NLT*). Give help, give the Gospel, and give yourself to prayer for them. Remember, I forgave those who crucified Me: "Father forgive them" (Luke 23:34, *NKJV*). Learn to minister in many ways.

Lord, I want to give to others just as others gave to me. But I want to do more to minister to others than they ministered to me. I want to minister as You ministered. Amen.

READING: Luke 6:27-38; Romans 12:17-21

KEY THOUGHT: Minister to the physical needs of those who are not My followers, even those who persecute My followers.

I AM JESUS—*Exponential Ministry*

"You have filled all Jerusalem with your teaching about Him."
ACTS 5:28, NLT

"Publically from house to house."
ACTS 20:20, NLT

Did you see the pattern in the early church? They were saturating their city with My teaching. Exponential ministry is serving people at every available time, with every available means or methods, to reach everyone available. That means start early, minister all day, and finish late. It means using more than one area of service, going to more than just one group of people. This is a picture of revival because they served in the power of the Holy Spirit. Also, it is a picture of exponential ministry. When your church is unselfish, you are a testimony to Me and the way I do ministry.

Lord, move me out of my comfort zone. My selfishness keeps me from helping a lot of people. Lord give me "Jesus eyes" to see the millions as You see them. Give me "Jesus hands" to serve as You ministered. Amen.

When you are saturating your neighborhood with ministry, you are giving exponential ministry. Not only are you sacrificing your time and giving resources, you are identifying with Me. Remember, I serve sacrificially, which means My example will motivate you to ministry. One way to judge if your ministry is exponential, look at your hands: do you have anything left? Also, look at your feet: have you gone everywhere to minister? Look into your heart: do you have any compassion that you have withheld? Then I will say, "Well done good and faithful servant. I will have much reward for you in heaven" (Matt. 25:21, ELT).

Lord, use my hands to help the needy. Use my feet to take me to those who need help. Fill my heart with gratitude to You. Amen.

READING: Acts 20:16-37

KEY THOUGHT: Another word for exponential is *saturation*. It is giving all types of ministry and all your energy, all the time to do as much as you can do.

I AM JESUS—*Your Example in Ministry*

"People were brought out into the streets on beds and mats . . . crowds came from . . .
around Jerusalem bringing their sick . . . all were healed."

ACTS 5:15-16, NLT

I am Jesus who serves others through your hands and your sacrificial service. There was exponential ministry because "More and more people believed and were brought to the Lord" (Acts 5:14, *NLT*). When you and your church give more than expected by the crowd, expect exponential results: "Believers were added to the Lord" (Acts 5:14). Isn't that what you desire and pray for and minister for? If your church doesn't have many lost people coming to get saved, then you and other church members must go out to where they are located. Do what? Give a "cup of water to drink in My name" (Mark 9:41, *NKJV*). The secret of exponential ministry is not what you can do, but what you can give. What will you give?

Lord, I bring My selfish heart to You. Heal it and transform it.
Give me Your heart for ministry and I will follow Your example of serving
in Your name. Amen.

Make your assembly a serving church to needs, no matter who and where and when. You cannot help everyone, but you can have a heart for all. You cannot do all types of service, but you can start with what you can do. If you—and all others in your church—begin serving other people, you will be amazed what multiple hands can do, and how much they can accomplish. And you will be amazed at the multiple times you are ministering.

Lord, the problem with humble service is not location or ability to serve.
The issue is my inner desire. I am selfish by nature. Forgive me and lead me
to a task I can do for You. Amen.

READING: Mark 9:33-41; Acts 5:1-16

KEY THOUGHT: Your example in ministry is Jesus who ministered in many ways, at many times, doing many types of humanitarian service.

I AM JESUS—*Serving People*

"But among you it will be different.
Whoever wants to be a leader among you must be your servant."

MARK 10:43, *NLT*

I came to serve people; follow My example. Serve other believers and serve those who are lost. Why? First, because the nature of love is giving, and I gave all for people. I serve because I love them, both My followers and those who do not follow Me. Ask the Father to give you a divine love. Second, serving is My nature. Notice how Paul described Me: "Though He was God . . . He gave up His divine privileges; He took the humble position of a slave" (Phil. 2:6-7, *NLT*). Ask the Father to give you a serving heart. But there is a third reason: because others are in need. The world is full of needy people. By ministering you open them up to salvation, and you actually alleviate their pain. They need you.

Lord, I want to minister to other people as You did. But serving is not always natural. I want my way and I want my needs satisfied, and I want it on my time Forgive me, cleanse me, and change me. Serve me so I can serve others. Amen.

At the Last Supper, "I got up . . . took off My robe . . . poured water into a basin . . . began to wash the disciple's feet" (John 13:4-5, *NLT*). Remember, they had just been arguing over who was the greatest. When I asked you to follow Me, I invited you, "Deny yourself, and take up your cross daily" (Luke 9:23, *ELT*). My example should motivate you to exponential serving. That is going beyond what a human could do; it's divine motivation.

Lord, I will follow Your example. I will serve others. Even when I don't want to, that is the time I will do it. Even when I think the task is too demeaning, I will do it just as You did. Amen.

READING: John 13:1-10

KEY THOUGHT: You must follow Jesus' example of serving when your example will help others, just as Jesus gave an example.

I AM JESUS—A Whole Healthy Ministering Body

"He makes the whole body fit together perfectly. As each part does its own special work, it helps the other parts grow, so that the whole body is healthy and growing and full of love."

EPHESIANS 4:16, *NLT*

I live in you and all other members of your local church so that My body is healthy, growing and possesses the divine attributes of love. Look at the phrase "helps the other parts grow." Have you ever thought that your growth in ministry will help others in your church grow? Sometimes you will have a direct ministry to them, such as teaching, counseling, or actually serving them. At other times you will work alongside them so they are motivated by your example. At other times, you may not touch their lives directly; they may not even know you; but as you make the body stronger, they benefit. When the water level is raised in a lake, all the boats on the lake go up. Ask God to make your ministry helpful to others.

Lord, I love to serve You in ministry; You are my primary motivation. But I also love my church and its people. Help me minister effectively to individuals and to the whole church. I want my spiritual gifts used, and I want Your body to grow. Amen.

You serve in ministry because you are motivated by your spiritual gifts (abilities). These gifts make you effective in ministry. But also My love will move you to action. Then there are many other motivations for serving Me. Remember, serving is not the main thing, nor are results the main motivation. It is your relationship with Me. You minister because "I am in you, and you are in Me" (John 14:20, *ELT*). When you strengthen your relationship with Me, your ministry will grow and be strengthened.

Lord, I serve others because of You.
Use my ministry to help others serve You better. Amen.

READING: Eph. 4:1-16; 1 Cor. 12:1-31

KEY THOUGHT: Jesus wants all in His body to serve as best as possible so they will grow peacefully and the body will grow completely.

I AM JESUS— *Using Every Available Person*

"Then the church . . . became stronger as the believers . . . with the encouragement of the Holy Spirit . . . grew in numbers."

ACTS 9:31, *NLT*

There are three principles in today's verse that should encourage you and all other followers of Me in your local church. First, all believers from all churches were encouraged in their ministry by the Holy Spirit. Not just the pastor and apostles, but "believers." So pray that you and all others in your church will have a fruitful ministry. Second, it took all—leaders and followers—to strengthen a church. If members in your church are not involved in ministry, then those weak links weaken the entire church. Third, new believers were saved and added to the church, and at the same time, new churches were being planted and the Great Commission was being fulfilled.

Lord, I don't want to be a weak link in the chain of ministry in my church. Show me what to do and what more I can do in my present ministry. Then use me in ministry and use my example to encourage others in their ministry. Amen.

My goal for your church is to involve every member, each doing their ministry to serve every need at all places and all times. When that happens, your church will grow and each member will grow in Christ. Then exponential ministry will produce exponential growth.

Lord, I pray to grow to maturity as I serve in ministry for You. I also pray that my church would grow to involve more in ministry and may my church grow in strength and outreach. Amen.

READING: Acts 9:20-31; Eph. 4:1-16

KEY THOUGHT: Jesus wants everyone in the church to use their ministry, so each will grow to spiritual maturity and the whole body would also grow to complete the Great Commission.

WEEK SIX

I AM JESUS:
My Church Expectations

Your reading and prayers this week will focus on My expectations for My followers and My church. You will examine the powerful commands I give to My followers and what I expect them to do. Then you will examine My various ways the Great Commission will produce exponential growth. Just as the early church was aggressive in testifying its faith to the world, so too today your church can become an exponential body of believers; let's change the world. The secret is, when all members realize what they can do for Me, and they make a commitment to do it, they will see exceptional ministry. Together they will have exponential results.

I AM JESUS—*A* Church *Reaching* *Average* *People*

"God in his wisdom saw . . . the world would never know him through human wisdom . . . few of you were wise in the world's eyes or powerful, or wealthy . . . rather God chose to use the (weak) . . . things counted as nothing . . . by the wise."

1 CORINTHIANS 1:21, 27-28, NLT

I am Jesus who calls average people and strengthens them to be above average—exceptional. I don't always call those with the highest IQ or the most money or powerful positions. I empower common people to do extraordinary ministry. When an average follower leads a millionaire to Christ, it's not to get his/her money, but to save him/her from hell. Average people do it because of My love through them, My power through their testimony, and the supernatural life in the Word of God that transforms the unsaved. If I can use Gideon who was the least important in his family to defeat over 100,000 Midianties, what can I do with you?

Lord, I am not big in the world's eyes, and I am not important in the eyes of business, but I want You to use me. Help me get someone saved and influence others. Use me in a way greater than my ability. Amen.

I am Jesus who fills your life with My presence. Don't try to do it by yourself. Let Me work through you. Let My light shine through your words, and actions. Focus on Me—not yourself—and I can use you to change one person or one family. Do you think you could change a neighborhood? Or more?

Lord, all I have to offer You is my life, my mind, my love, and my desire to serve You. Come forgive my sin and overcome my weaknesses. Fill me with the Holy Spirit's power and give me opportunities to serve You. Amen.

READING: Acts 6:1-6; 8:4-40

KEY THOUGHT: I use ordinary followers to do extraordinary things through their yieldedness and My power.

Day 37

I AM JESUS—*A Church of All Nationalities*

"Some . . . began preaching . . . only to Jews. However the church in Antioch . . . preached to the Gentiles . . . a large number of Gentiles believed."

ACTS 11:20-21, *ELT*

"It doesn't matter if you are a Jew, or a Gentile . . . barbaric, uncivilized, slave, or free. Christ . . . lives in all of us."

COLOSSIANS 3:11, *NLT*

I am a church made up of men, women, children and all cultures of the world. The children sing a chorus in Sunday school, "Red and yellow, black or white, they are precious in His sight." That is the essence of My New Testament church. Because everyone is in Me, they are in My church. I live in people of every ethnic race, and through them I reach their family, friends, and neighbors. Have I reached you and your family? If so, I want to work through you to evangelize all your relationships. You may be the only one who can lead them to salvation. If you don't do it, who else can I use?

Lord, thank You for my salvation, and thank You for those who brought the Gospel to my family. I pray for everyone in my family to become a Christian—young and old—men and women—all of them. Use me to reach people with the Gospel that no one else could do. Amen.

I am a church made up of all cultures of the world. When you get to heaven I invite you to join in the choir to sing hallelujah and praise to the Father. What culture are you from? You will join all people from every tribe (ethnic group) and language, all with a color different from yours and a language different from you—will you be comfortable in My heaven?

Lord, I love Your church of many colors and many language, and many cultures. I pray for the Gospel to reach every tribe in the world. Help me to do my part to carry the Gospel to the ends of the earth. Amen.

READING: Gal. 3:26-27; Rev. 5:8-10

KEY THOUGHT: I commanded the Gospel to be preached to every tribe (ethnic group) until all groups have heard the Gospel.

I AM JESUS—*A Church of the Rich and Poor*

"Joseph . . . nicknamed Barnabas . . . from the tribe of Levi . . . came from the island of Cyprus. He sold a field he owned and brought the money to the apostles."

ACTS 5:36-37, NLT

I am a church made up of all kinds of people—rich and poor—from all different places. One of the first missionaries was Barnabas, who owned a field but sold it and gave all the money to Me. He remembered what I told the rich young ruler: "One thing you haven't done. sell all your possessions and give the money to the poor" (Luke 18:22, *NLT*). Barnabas did that, and the apostles used that money to give to the poor. When a person sacrifices everything to Me, I can use them, like I did Barnabas. It is not wrong to possess money; it is wrong for money to possess you. Remember the man who had five bags of silver (Matt. 25:16). When he used his money properly for My purpose, I commanded him and gave him five more bags. The one who had only one bag of silver selfishly hoarded it and hid it. I took it away from him (Matt. 25:24-25). It's not wrong to have money and use it for My ministry. It is wrong when money has you.

Lord, forgive me for being selfish and stingy. I yield everything to You. Take control of all My money, possessions and "stuff." Use them for Your glory. Amen.

I am a church made up of rich and poor. Remember the widow woman giving her money in the temple. She didn't give a lot, "two small coins." Then I said, "She has given more . . . she has given everything she has" (Luke 21:2, 4, *NLT*). It is not what you give to Me; it is your attitude of humility. It is not how much you give; it is how much you hang on to after you give to Me.

Lord, You own everything—the earth, the cattle in the fields and the gold in the mines. I give You everything. Use it for Your purpose. Whatever You leave for me to use, I will spend it for Your glory. Amen.

READING: Luke 21:1-4; Matt. 25:14-30

KEY THOUGHT: There are different levels of income among My people in My church. They should surrender all to My use and use wisely what is left over for them.

I AM JESUS—A Unified Church Working

*"We will speak . . . growing in every way more and more like Christ,
who is the head of his body, the church."*

EPHESIANS 4:15, NLT

Iam Jesus, a unified body. When you plant Me in a neighborhood, lost people will be converted to become members of My body. Then each believer will grow in spiritual maturity, and as all grow together to be an effective body, they will minister in that neighborhood for Me. Like a physical body, they will work in coordinated unity. But each believer will have different spiritual gifts, different personalities, and different backgrounds. Each will bring different abilities to make My body effective. Again like a physical body, each member of the church body will work in mutual fellowship. Just as each member of a body gives different life to the whole body, so too each believer will contribute richness and variety to ministry. Then there is dependency, the little finger needs the arm to reach out, and they both need eyes to guide what they do. A small member like an ear needs a large member like a backbone.

Lord, everyone in my church is not like me, and they don't function like me and they don't have my priorities. Give me love for the uniqueness of each and for the strength of each. I will not criticize another; help me to see the good points in others that You see. Amen.

I am Jesus, the head of the body. I made everyone different in your church, but they all belong to Me and depend on Me just as you do. Keep your eyes on Me, your Lord. Keep giving 100 percent of your talents to carry out the Great Commission. Pray for others with different personalities, support others with different talents, and work with all to make this body healthy. Then all believers will worship the Father, bringing others to salvation, and helping build the spirituality of all.

Lord forgive me when I think only of my personal needs. Help me support my whole church body, love all members, and build up the weak and needy. Use my church as a body to complete the Great Commission. Amen.

READING: 1 Cor. 12:1-31

KEY THOUGHT: A church functions like a human body, and all parts of the body work together to accomplish the purpose of the body.

I AM JESUS—A Reaching Body

"And the church is His body, it is made full and complete by Christ, who fills all things everywhere with Himself."

EPHESIANS 1:23, *NLT*

I am Jesus, the Church body. When you plant a new church, you put Me in that culture. When it is located in a culture different from your previous church, or even different from the way you live, I can reach the people of that culture. I love the people of every culture in the world. Remember, I commissioned you, "Go and make disciples of all the nations," i.e., *ethna* means people groups (Matthew 28:19, *NLT*). Because every person from every culture is lost in sin (Rom. 3:23; 5:12), I want My church to be a soul-winning body in every culture. Because We, the Trinity, love every individual in every culture, I want you to be a loving church body to witness to them (Acts 1:8). Because I will save everyone in every people group in the world, I want you to be an inviting church body.

Lord, I know You created all the cultures of the world, and You died for everyone in every culture; give me a burden to pray for them to be saved. Give me a vision of praying for a church body—Your presence—to be planted in every culture. Amen.

I am Jesus, the living body that preaches the gospel to all. I want you to plant Me in every language group in the world. You cannot do it by yourself, but you and all My other followers can do it together. Come together, pray together, plan together, give money together, and help preach the gospel to every people group in the world: "And the Good News about the Kingdom will be preached throughout the whole world, so that all nations will hear it; and then the end will come" (Matt. 24:14, *NLT*).

Lord Jesus, I know You are the church and I am in You. Wake me up to my responsibility to get the gospel to every person in every culture in the world. I will pray, work, give money, and do my part. Help me. Amen.

READING: Matt. 28:16-20; 1 Thess. 1:1-10

KEY THOUGHT: The church is the body of Jesus and He must be planted in every culture of the world to live in that group of people to win them to salvation.

I AM JESUS— *Persecution Makes Me Execptional*

"Saul was going everywhere to destroy the church . . . house to house . . . to throw them into prison."

ACTS 8:3, NLT

"Saul! Saul! Why are you persecuting me . . . I am Jesus, the one you are persecuting!"

ACTS 9:4-5, NLT

When anyone attacks believers for their faith, they are attacking Me, the Lord Jesus, who is the Church. Did you see that truth in today's scripture? Saul was persecuting believers, going house to house to arrest and put them in prison. But it wasn't just people he was persecuting; he was attacking Me. Remember, I indwell every believer. So to harm a believer for their faith is to harm Me. When someone attacks your faith, don't get angry and don't get even. Pray for your critics as Stephen did when he was executed by stoning for his faith: "Lord, lay not this sin to their charge" (Acts 7:60, *NLT*). Then demonstrate your victorious Christian attitude (1 John 4:4). Also, your prayers may lead some to salvation.

Lord, forgive me when I have sinned by criticizing my church, or any church. I now pray for my church: protect it, use it, and make it strong against attacks. I pray the same for my faith: make me strong in the face of criticism or attacks. May I have a forgiving spirit. Amen.

When someone criticizes or attacks your church, they attack Me. Yes, I will forgive them when they repent, but you should never stoop to their level by dishing out to them what they dish out to you. I said, "Bless those who curse you. Pray for those who hurt you" (Luke 6:28, *NLT*). You may eventually get them to follow Me. Remember, Stephen prayed for his persecutor—Saul—and Saul was saved to become Paul, My greatest apostle to the Gentiles.

Lord, work on my attitude to make me sweet, and give me faith to believe You will convert my persecutors to salvation. Amen.

READING: Acts 7:50–8:4; 9:1-19

KEY THOUGHT: When anyone persecutes the church, they are attacking Jesus. The positive response of believers to persecution can lead to the salvation of the attackers.

I AM JESUS—*Living in My Church*

"For where two or three gather together as my followers, I am there among them."

MATTHEW 18:20, *NLT*

I am Jesus the Church, the true assembly of believers. My followers believe I am the Son of God and Son of man, i.e., the God-man who was born of a virgin, lived without sin, and died on a cross for their sins (John 1:29). Those in a local church body have committed themselves to follow Me (Mark 1:11-12). When they all come together, they enjoy My presence because I said, "Where two or three are gathered together in My name, I am there in the midst of them" (Matt. 18:20, *NKJV*). Some people may just attend your assembly or may even join your assembly. But if they don't believe in Me for salvation, they are not My followers. They are not part of the body of Christ (Eph. 1:22-23). An authentic body of Christ is not a building, organization or religious service held on Sundays. The authentic body of Christ is Me, and if you believe in Me, then you are in My universal body.

Lord, I have read about You in the Bible and believe You are who You say You are. You are my Savior. Thank You for giving me a hope to live with You in heaven forever. You are also my Lord; lead me today. Amen.

I am Jesus, the body of Christ. When you criticize the church, you are complaining about Me. When you don't attend on Sunday, I miss your worship. When you don't give your time, or your tithe, or your talents in service, My body doesn't grow. Remember, your faith is expressed in a dedicated relationship with Me.

Lord, teach me to reverence Your church as I reverence you. I love You with all my heart, I will serve You with all my talents, and I yield the control of all my "stuff" to You. I love You. Amen.

READING: Eph. 4:9-16

KEY THOUGHT: The church is Jesus; therefore, you should relate to your church as you would relate to Jesus.

WEEK SEVEN

I AM JESUS
Pictures of My Exponential Church

The church is a supernatural creation by God the Father who sent Me, His Son, to die for the sins of the world. I died on the cross for the sins of lost people. Now those who are saved are in My body—Jesus, the local church—to live for Me in the world. The night before I died, I promised, "You in Me, and I in you" (John 14:20, *NKJV*). All Christians were placed into Me on the cross and now I live in them. But the picture analogy continues; today a believer is a member of My local church body. At the same time I am in the believer, ministering to the lost world through them in My church.

I AM JESUS—*The Church's Many Pictures*

"So now you Gentiles are no longer strangers and foreigners. You are citizens along with all of God's holy people. You are members of God's family. Together, we are his house, built on the foundation of the apostles and the prophets. And the cornerstone is Christ Jesus himself. We are carefully joined together in him, becoming a holy temple for the Lord. Through him you Gentiles are also being made part of this dwelling where God lives by his Spirit."

EPHESIANS 2:19-22, *NLT*

I am Jesus, the Church (Eph. 1:22-23). But did you see My other church names in today's reading? I am called "the household of God," so everyone in My house is family; you are called a child of God. Notice, you are no longer strangers or foreigners, but a fellow citizen and a member of the family. My church is also called a *Temple*, and I am the cornerstone of that sanctuary. When I come into your life at salvation (Eph. 3:17), you also were placed into Me. Paul frequently calls this "in Christ." "At that day you will know that . . . you (are) in Me, and I in you" (John 14:20, *NKJV*). So, the church is a household; and you are in Me.

Lord, I love my church because I love You. I come seeking Your presence when I worship. But more than that, I want Your presence with me 24/7. Amen.

Don't think of your church as an organization, or meetings with programs. I am the Church, and today's reading says it is "this dwelling where God lives" (Eph. 2:22, *NLT*). The church is My body and My life. Next, it is the dwelling place of the Father, and His majesty and glory live there. Then the Holy Spirit indwells the church (1 Cor. 3:16). My church has met in caves, in mountains, and catacombs under the city of Rome. My church has met in tents, under the open sky, and in some of the most beautiful structures in the world. But those were only outward buildings. The church meets where My presence dwells.

Lord, I will go to church to meet You. It is not about friends or a position where I serve, and it's not about habit. It's all about You. Since You indwell me, I will live in Your church. Amen.

READING: Eph. 2:14-22; 1 Cor. 3:9-23

KEY THOUGHT: The church has many names; today's lesson pictures Jesus as the dwelling place where the church assembles.

I AM JESUS—My Church the Bride

"The bride, the Lamb's wife."
DEUTERONOMY 21:9, NKJV

"You as a pure bride to one husband—Christ."
2 CORINTHIANS 11:2, NLT

The church is pictured as My bride. A bride is beautiful to the groom; all those who are saved are beautiful to Me because I first loved them. Just as a bride gives herself to her husband, so to you must give yourself to Me. You will do that because you love Me. It will be easy to love Me when you realize how much I love you. How much is that? I gave Myself in death to forgive your sins. The key ingredient in a marriage relationship is love. Keep our relationship open, growing, and warm. Love is the greatest quality in life. Love me as I love you.

Lord, forgive me when I sin against You and Your love. Cleanse me and restore me to intimate fellowship. I want to serve You because I love You and because You love me. You have given me eternal life and everlasting fellowship. Make me worthy of Your love. Amen.

Just as a bride must be pure for her husband, so to I want you to be holy, separated from sin to Me. Just as a bride lives with her husband, you will live forever with Me. Just as a bride forsakes all others for her husband, turn your back on all religions, and all the gods of all religions. I am Jesus, the Son of God; I am your only way to the heavenly Father (John 14:6).

Lord, I give myself completely to You from this day forward to do everything You want me to do. Because we are one (John 14:20), I will follow You, serve You and love You. Amen.

READING: Rev. 19:7-10; Eph. 5:23-32

KEY THOUGHT: The Bible describes the church as a bride, so the church must relate to Christ just as a bride relates to her husband.

Day 45

I AM JESUS—*Shepherd of My Flock*

"Guard yourselves and God's people. Feed and shepherd God's flock—his church, purchased with his own blood . . . I know that false teachers, like vicious wolves, will come in . . . not sparing the flock."

ACTS 20:28-29, NLT

My church is like a flock of sheep that needs human shepherds—pastors—to tend to them. I am the Chief Shepherd (1 Pet. 5:4), and My pastors are under-shepherds. A flock needs three things: (1) tending or leading, because sheep cannot lead themselves, (2) feeding, a shepherd finds green pastures, and (3) protection, a flock must be guarded from false teachers who will lead them astray and from diseases like sin that will destroy them. I am Jesus, your Shepherd; stay close to Me, so I can lead, feed, and protect you.

Lord, You are my Shepherd, I will lay down in Your green pastures, lead me beside still cool spiritual waters to restore my soul. Protect me when I walk through the valley of the shadow of death (Ps. 23:1-4). Amen.

You are My church, the flock for whom I gave Myself (John 10:11). As an earthly shepherd loves his sheep, so I love you and all others in your church. Because of that, I am the Shepherd who goes out in the storm to find lost sheep in the wilderness (Luke 15:3-7). One day I will return from heaven to take you and every one of My sheep to live with Me forever: "When the Chief Shepherd appears, you will receive the crown of glory" (1 Pet. 5:4).

Lord, You prepare a table of food to feed me, and You anoint my head and bruises with oil, and You give me a cup that is filled to the brim. Thank You for being my Shepherd (Ps. 23:4-6). Amen.

READING: Ps. 23:1-6; John 10:1-18

KEY THOUGHT: My church is called a flock and My believers are called sheep. I will look after them like the Shepherd of Psalm 23.

60

I AM JESUS—A Church Garden

"I [Paul] planted the seed in your hearts, and Apollos watered it, but it was God who made it grow . . . the one who plants and the one who waters work together . . . for we are both God's workers. And you are God's field."

1 CORINTHIANS 3:6, 8-9, *NLT*

I am Jesus the church, which is described as a garden. The focus is individuals growing in Christian faith and inner character. But also the church body is growing in attendance, evangelistic outreach, numbers and love. The church is shown as a field or trees (Israel is an olive or fig tree and the church is a vine), or a farm to produce a harvest of fruit or the beauty of flowers. The church is a cultivated plot of ground where weeds and rocks are removed, seed is sown, and plants are cared for until the harvest. What do these pictures tell you? You must depend on Me alone as the source of life, growth and harvest. I said, "Abide in Me, and I in you. As the branch cannot bear fruit of itself, unless it abides in the vine, neither can you, unless you abide in Me" (John 15:4, *NKJV*).

Lord, help me grow to produce fruit for Your glory. I am different from all other seeds in the church garden. Help Me produce fruit both in character growth and winning the lost. I want my fruit to satisfy hungry and needy people. Amen.

Did you see that double transference? "You abide in Me and I abide in you." At salvation I enter your heart to give you eternal life. Then you must abide in Me to keep growing and producing fruit. You abide in Me by prayer, obeying My words in Scripture, serving and ministering to others. But most of all by intimate fellowship and worship. Don't get cut off from Me like a withered-up branch lying on the ground.

Lord, I will abide in You so Your life-giving energy can flow into my life. It is peaceful when I am close to You, letting fruit grow in my life. I want to get closer to You to produce more fruit. Amen.

READING: 1 Cor. 3:5-9; John 15:1-8

KEY THOUGHT: My church is like a garden where plants (people) grow to produce fruit.

Day 47

I AM JESUS—*A Growing Temple*

"I [Paul] have laid the foundation . . . now others are building it.
No one can lay any foundation other than—Jesus Christ . . . all of you together are
the temple of God and that the Spirit of God lives in you."

1 CORINTHIANS 3:10-11, 16, *NLT*

I am Jesus, a living temple. Each of you is a part of the construction material. Some are gold, silver, jewels, wood, hay and stubble. When you get to heaven it will be revealed what kind of construction stone you are (3:13). Some will be rewarded; others will have their works burned up (3:14-15). So strive to be pure, diligent and worthy, because you are My temple, and I want you and My church to be holy.

Lord, thank You for making me a part of Your church—you body. Forgive any
and all of my sin; cleanse me. I will live a holy life to please You and serve You.
Amen.

I build a temple to dwell in. After all the workers finished Solomon's Temple, it was beautiful, gold plated, and magnificent to the eye. But its real beauty was when the Father, I and the Holy Spirit indwelt it: "A thick cloud filled the temple . . . the glorious presence of the Lord filled the Temple of God" (2 Chron. 5:13-14, *NLT*). Let Me fill your life; you will be a beautiful temple and people will see My presence in your life.

Lord, come dwell in my life. Fill my mind with Your presence.
Quiet my emotions to love and worship You, bend my will to serve You.
Come make Your home in my heart. Amen.

READING: 1 Cor. 3:10-17; 2 Chron. 5:1-14

KEY THOUGHT: My church is a temple where I live. Build it to be beautiful and functional, because I will come indwell it.

Day 48

I AM JESUS—*A Church of Priests*

*"You are a chosen generation, a royal priesthood, a holy people . . .
show the praises to Him who called you."*
1 PETER 2:9, *NKJV*

"Let us continually offer the sacrifice of praise to God, that is, the fruit of our lips."
HEBREWS 13:15, *NKJV*

My Old Testament priest offered the sacrifice of blood to Me as a symbol of cleansing and forgiveness. But I am the Priest who offered My blood for the world (1 Tim. 2:5). Now My church is made up of priests—every believer—who offer the sacrifices of worship and praise. Have you done that today? Because I—your High Priest—saved your soul, you should continually offer praise and worship to God the Father.

Lord I come to You—my High Priest—thanking You for my salvation, and for complete cleansing from all sin (1 John 1:9). Now I offer praises and worship for Your extraordinary gift of salvation. Amen.

You are a priest. You should pray daily for yourself, conferring your sin (1 John 1:4), and seeking to grow spiritually. Second, you should intercede for believers, rulers, and My workers to carry out the Great Commission around the world (1 Tim. 2:1). Then you should worship and praise the Father, Holy Spirit and Me in worship.

Lord, I ask forgiveness for my failure to be your priest, doing what You require. I pray for all people everywhere (1 Tim. 2:1-5). Next, I intercede for the salvation of lost family and friends. Finally I offer You worship—the sacrifice of my lips and words. Be glorified in me, in my church and the world. Amen.

READING: I Pet. 2:1-15; 1 Tim. 2:1-8

KEY THOUGHT: My church is a priesthood, and each member is a priest who intercedes and offers worship to the Father.

63

I AM JESUS—*A Church of People Different*

*"The human body has many parts, but the many parts make up one whole body.
So it is with the body of Christ."*

1 CORINTHIANS 12:12, *NLT*

"Bodies have many parts and God has put each part just where He wants it."

1 CORINTHIANS 12:19, *NLT*

My church is called a body, which is made up of lots of different people—men, women and children. But each person is part of the body, just like your body has arms, eyes, feet, etc. Just as each part of your physical body must work in harmony with the whole, every believer must work in harmony with all others. Can you sing, speak, counsel, or give lots of money? Serve your church body where you are strongest and can do the most good. Can you pray, serve, or teach? I want every believer in My church to sacrifice and work hard; let's change the world!

Lord, I am not the best in my church. Some people sing better than me, whereas I can sing better than a few others. Use me—use all of us—to glorify You in music. I don't want to be in competition with others; I want to cooperate with them. Amen.

My body is different in various cultures. Some churches are in the jungle, others in suburbia, and still others in skyscrapers in metropolitan areas. Different churches reach different kinds of people. Some of My churches are strong in teaching, while others are strong in worship—exaltation—and still others have practical preaching. And then some churches meet in small groups like underground churches. Find out your strength and use it for your church to reach lost people. Find out the strength of your church and support its outreach. Let's change the world.

Lord, thank You for my church, for the way they worship and serve and care for one another. May I care for them as much as You care for them. Amen.

READING: 1 Cor. 12:1-31

KEY THOUGHT: The church is a unified body, yet its members are different in age, talent, background, training, and spiritual gifts. All must work together to carry out the Great Commission.

Your 50th Day of Prayer

I have talked to you in 7 weekly devotionals, telling you how My church will change the world. Now we come to the 50th devotional. It is all about the end—the Great Commission is completed. This lesson is about the Omegan—the one person somewhere on Earth who will hear the gospel (could be man, woman or child) and will accept salvation. Omega means the last, as alpha means the first. When the last person is saved, immediately the Father will send Me to go gather My church—living and dead—the Great Commission is completed. At least one person from every *ethne* tribe has become a follower of Me. What will you do to reach the Omegan? I know that Elmer Towns prays daily that one of his students will reach the Omegan for salvation.

I AM JESUS—*Looking for Omegan*

"And the Good News about the Kingdom will be preached throughout the whole world, so that all nations will hear it; and then the end will come."

MATTHEW 24:14, *NLT*

I am Jesus who gave you the Great Commission to evangelize every tribe on Earth. You are to witness as effectively as possible, to as many people as possible, for as long as possible. When will the task be finished, and when will you be done? The answer is simple. When the gospel has been preached in every people group (Gk. *ethne* or culture). Some have called the last person to be saved Omegan. This name comes from the Greek alphabet, beginning with the letter Alpha and ending with Omega. When the last person believes for salvation, the Father will say to Me, "Go get Our people and bring them home." Then I will come to rapture all My followers to heaven. The dead in Christ will be caught up first (1 Thess. 4:16). Then those who are alive will instantly follow them to heaven (1 Thess. 4:17).

Lord, I am ready for Your return. I am saved and ready to go.
But I have unsaved friends and family. Help me reach them with the message
before it is too late. I pray for their salvation. Amen.

I am Jesus who will transform your bodies and I will take you to heaven. Just as you were transformed inwardly when you were saved, you will then have a new body as I rapture you to be with Me. Your old sinful nature in the future will be gone. You will know Me and all others as you are known (1 John 3:2). You will join the massive worshiping choir before the throne, singing, "You are worthy, O Lord our God, to receive glory and honor and power" (Rev. 4:11, *NLT*).

Lord, I look forward to that instant when You transform me into a likeness like
Yourself. But while I am on the earth, use me to win lost people to You.
I will work because of the Day of Your coming. Amen.

READING: Matt. 24:1-14; Rev. 4:1-11

KEY THOUGHT: The Great Commission will be finished when the gospel is preached to the last culture (*ethne*) and the last person is saved.

I Am
Jesus
Let's Change the World

MY **EXCEPTIONAL** FOLLOWERS

MAKE AN **EXPONENTIAL** CHURCH

ELMER L. TOWNS

CONTENTS

PART ONE

I AM JESUS: LET'S CHANGE THE WORLD

INTRODUCTION

I am Jesus—the Church. The Bible identified the church as My body, "The church is his body; it is made full and complete by Christ" (Eph. 1:23, *NLT*). I am the Church made up of My followers, "Where two or three gather together as my followers, I am there among them" (Matt. 18:20, *NLT*). So, how do I grow since I am Jesus? The church ought to grow as I did as a young boy: "Jesus grew in wisdom and in stature and in favor with God and all the people" (Luke 2:52, *NLT*).

As a boy I grew in four areas: (1) intellectual ability, (2) physical measurement, (3) spiritually before the Father, and (4) socially according to the expectations of all the people.

Therefore, My local churches ought to grow in these same four areas. First, my local church must grow in knowledge of the Scriptures, doctrinal understanding and wisdom of divine growth principles, i.e., exponential growth (that growing according to the formula of the Great Commission).

Second, My church should grow in stature, through observable measures of baptisms, of members, of attendance, of offerings, and people involved in ministry.

Third, My church should grow in faith with the heavenly Father; this is spiritual growth—that means individual growth in prayer and fasting, with growth of corporate prayer and fasting. Also, members should individually grow spiritually. The local body should grow more spiritual in all their outward relationships and duties. All should seek fellowship with Me, intimacy with one another, and all should worship both the Father and Me (John 4:23, 24).

Finally, My local body should grow socially with the community as they serve the needs of both individuals and the neighborhoods where they live.

Just as I grew from a tiny infant into full manhood, My local body must grow exponentially into a full local church body that glorifies the Father in heaven and has a good testimony with all outside the church.

FOREWORD

I AM JESUS: LET'S CHANGE THE WORLD

I am Jesus who comes to live in your life at salvation. In this book you will learn the importance of becoming My exceptional follower so that you fellowship together with others in an exponential church. The Father in heaven sent Me to be born of a virgin—without sin. I lived a perfect life—without sin. Even though satan tempted Me to obey him and reject who I was, I didn't sin; I won that victory over him. On the cross I died for the sins of the world—your sins. I won the victory for all who will put their faith in Me; I give them eternal life. Now I want you to grow in your faith to become an exceptional follower who reaches out to the lost.

AN EXCEPTIONAL FOLLOWER

An exceptional Christian is one who grows to love Me with "all their heart, soul and mind" (Matt. 22:37, *NLT*). The word *exceptional* means extraordinary, or remarkable, or unexpected. I want you to be transformed and live for greater goals (Phil. 3:10-14), to be motivated with greater desires (Phil. 4:14), and let the gospel light shine through you to others (Phil. 2:16). I want you to be exceptional in your life and service.

AN EXPONENTIAL CHURCH

When you come together with other Christians, I am there: "For where two or three gather together as my followers, I am there among them" (Matt. 18:20, *NLT*). That gathering is also called My body (Eph. 1:22-23). So when you see an assembly (the Greek word *church* means assembly), you are looking at Me and you can see My influence through them. The main task of a church is the Great Commission, "Go into all the world and preach the Good News to everyone" (Mark 16:15, *NLT*). That is your task.

Exponential means rapid increase in all areas according to a pre-determined formula. The Great Commission was the predetermined formula, the Holy Spirit was the source of increase, and the result was Me—a living, growing body efficient in ministry that exhibits all the strengths that a church was predicted to become.

Notice that the 7 chapters in this book all have to do with exceptional followers making an exponential church.

EXCEPTIONAL BELIEVERS MAKE MY CHURCH EXPONENTIAL

50 DAYS OF DEVOTIONS

I died on the cross on the Jewish Passover, and I arose on the third day. During the next 50 days I was equipping My disciples to carry out the Great Commission. I want to equip you and members in your church to do the same thing. After 50 days of waiting and pray-ing, the Holy Spirit came upon the church on the day of Pentecost (Pentecost means fifty). Immediately, My church began winning people with the gospel, so much so that the enemy accused it of "turning the world upside down" (Acts 17:6).

Now I want to talk to you in 50 daily devotionals that are included at the end of this book. These devotionals will challenge you to an exponential ministry of outreach.

Then there are daily prayers so that you can talk to Me. You will pray for a burden for lost people and a vision of what I can do in your life and through your church. You will pray for your leaders, fellow workers, and the total outreach of your church. It will be an exciting 50 days—if you and your people ask for a great victory.

PART ONE

I Am
Jesus
Let's Change the World

I AM JESUS:

A Church Growing Exponentially

> *"He makes the whole body fit together perfectly. As each part does its own special work, it helps the other parts grow, so that the whole body is healthy and growing and full of love."*

EPHESIANS 4:16, *NLT*

Because I, Jesus, gave the commission to preach the Gospel to every person, the exponential church aggressively carried out My command. Because I promised to give whatsoever asked in My name, a growing church fulfilled My promise. Because I promised "anyone who believes in me will do the same works I have done, and even greater works" (John 14:12, *NLT*), an evangelistic church became a reality. Because the exponential church saturates its area with the gospel, going everywhere to "turn the world upside down" (Acts 17:6), it becomes a greater challenge for all churches to be *exponential* in all they are and to reach the world for Christ.

Exponential means rapid increase in all areas according to a predetermined formula. The Great Commission was that formula, the Holy Spirit was the source of increase, and the result was a rapidly growing congregation efficient in all ministry that exhibits all that Christianity was predicted to become.

EXPONENTIAL EVANGELISM

The early church practiced *exponential evangelism*, filling Jerusalem with the gospel. Their enemies accused them, "Did we not strictly command you not to teach in this name? And look, you have filled Jerusalem with your doctrine" (Acts 5:28, *NKJV*). They filled their Jerusalem with the gospel, so must you. Your "Jerusalem" is that area the Holy Spirit has laid upon your heart. Those are the people you must saturate with the gospel. Sometimes your Jerusalem will be larger than the immediate neighborhood around your church. To some, your Jerusalem is your county; to others your Jerusalem is your state. Then others will have a Jerusalem that is greater than one state; it may be many states or nations.

How can you fill your "Jerusalem" with the gospel? The following definition was used by Jerry Falwell to describe how he got the job done: "Preaching the gospel to every available person, by every available means, at every available time."[1]

EXPONENTIAL VISION

Jerry Falwell first came to Lynchburg, Virginia, to start Thomas Road Baptist Church. He eventually built the 9th largest church in America. His vision was the secret of God's success through him. He posted a map on the back wall of his small church auditorium and drew a circle representing one mile in circumference around the church. He determined to visit every single home within that one-mile area. Beginning at 9:00 AM each morning, and working late into the evening, he visited every home with the purpose of (1) inviting them to church, (2) leaving a testimony of Christ, (3) offering to help them spiritually, and (4) when possible, attempting to lead someone to Jesus Christ. When he finished the first one-mile circumference, he extended his circle to two miles, then three miles, and before long, the circle included the whole city of Lynchburg, and then the surrounding counties. Then through television and radio, he extended his Jerusalem to the state of Virginia; next the United States, and then the world. His Jerusalem began with Lynchburg but eventually encompassed the world. Why did his congregation work so hard with him? One of the first laws of leadership states, "When followers buy into your vision, they will follow your leadership." You must pray for the Father to give you an *exponential vision* for your Jerusalem. As I help you evangelize your Jerusalem, your church can grow just as large as your vision.

EXPONENTIAL PRAYING

Originally, there were 120 people in the Upper Room praying for power to fulfill the Great Commission: "Peter stood up in the midst of the disciples, and said, (the number of names together were about a hundred and twenty)" (Acts 1:15). The early church grew because of *exponential praying*. Just praying is not enough to saturate your Jerusalem with the gospel; you must use *exponential* praying. What was this? In the church in Jerusalem, "They were all praying" (Acts 2:1), "They were all in one accord" (Acts 2:1), "They were all in one place" (Act 2:1), and "They were all filled with the Holy Spirit" (Acts 2:4). *Exponential vision* leads to *exponential prayer* that will result in *exponential evangelism*. That means (1) getting everyone to pray for spiritual power, (2) getting everyone to come together for prayer, and (3) getting focused prayer for evangelism. Also remember all the disciples were praying, all the men were praying, and all the women were praying.

EXPONENTIAL GROWTH

Peter preached a very simple sermon on the day of Pentecost, a sermon that can be read in less than four minutes. As a result, "They that gladly received his word were baptized: and the same day there were added unto them about three thousand souls" (Acts 2:41). In one day the church jumped from 120 people to over 3,000 people. That's *exponential growth*.

The next numerical indication of growth in the Jerusalem church was, "Howbeit many of them which heard the word believed; and the number of the men was about five thousand" (Acts 4:4). Now this is not just 5,000 Christians. The Greek word for "men" is not mankind, but males. The new converts represented 5,000 heads of households. Just as the men who were heads of households were counted in the book of Numbers, so the Jerusalem Church made up of mostly Jews counted the same way. So, with 5,000 men, there were 5,000 wives, and probably 2 to 4 children per family; so, there was a church of 20-30,000 converts. That's *exponential blessing*.

Next, the church had *exponential expansion*. So many were being saved that they no longer counted with exact numeric numbers, "And believers were the more added to the Lord, multitudes both of men and women" (Acts 5:14). Instead of using exact figures to measure this new growing church, they described it as a "multitude." When you have *exponential expansion*, it means both men and women. Why did they stop posting attendance figures? Because there were so many new converts in this church, they couldn't count them. Like massive demonstrations when multitudes gather, there were so many—they just couldn't count them.

EXPONENTIAL TEACHING

Next, there was *exponential teaching*. Notice what the 3,120 new converts did: "They continued steadfastly in the apostles' doctrine" (Acts 2:42) (the word *doctrine* in the *King James* is the verb for teaching, as seen in another modern versions), and "All the believers devoted themselves to the apostles' teaching" (Acts 2:42, *NLT*). If you want to have an *exponential church*, you must have *exponential teaching* of the Word of God. How is that done? (1) You must continue teaching as the Jerusalem church did, which means every day individuals were studying scripture, every day at the family altar, every Sunday in the church, i.e., all times with all methods. (2) You must teach the whole Bible from Genesis 1:1 to Revelation 22:21. (3) Next, you must teach the Scriptures "steadfastly," which means you teach with confidence and with purpose. Then you are *exponentially teaching* the Bible, which means you are confident that it is the inspired Word of God that will transform lives. *Exponential teaching* is instructing even if no other church teaches and instructing when you don't want to teach.

EXPONENTIAL FELLOWSHIP

Next, the early church had *exponential fellowship*. This does not mean drinking a lot of coffee or eating a lot of donuts together. No! See how *exponential fellowship* was practiced in the early church, "And all that believed were together" (Acts 2:44). It means they all attended services at the same time. You can't have an *exponential church* if some members are absent and other members are not regular in attendance. When some members choose not to attend worship services, they reflect a lack of spirituality. The early church was a gathered church, "And they, continuing daily with one accord in the temple, and breaking bread from house to house" (Acts 2:46). *Exponential fellowship* means Christians coming together on a face-to-face basis in (1) regular attendance, (2) making church worship a priority over personal pursuits, (3) attending church to obey God's Word, and (4) using their spiritual gifts in service through the church. *Exponential fellowship* means desiring to fellowship with your church to do everything I want you to do when Christians meet together.

EXPONENTIAL WORSHIP

Because I was in the midst of the church, they had *exponential worship*. What were Christians doing? "Praising God" (Acts 2:47). I had told the Samaritan woman, "The Father seeks worshippers" (John

4:23, *NLT*). Because the Father wants My people to worship Him, an *exponential church* has *exponential worship*. Worship is defined as "giving God the worthship that is due to Him." When you *exponentially praise* the Father, you pour out your appreciation to Him. When you *exponentially exalt* the Father, you put Him at the pinnacle of your life. When you *exponentially magnify* the Father, you give Him the "largest" place in your life. When you *exponentially worship* the Father, you give Him everything in your life.

EXPONENTIAL BOLDNESS

The Jewish Sanhedrin threatened the Christians in Jerusalem against speaking in My name, but Christians continued witnessing and sharing the gospel. They didn't stop ministering because of their opposition. When threatened, the entire church went to prayer: "Lord, behold their threatenings: and grant unto thy servants, that with all boldness they may speak thy word" (Acts 4:29).

How did I respond to their prayers? "When they had prayed, the place was shaken where they were assembled together; and they were all filled with the Holy Spirit and spake the word of God with boldness" (Acts 4:31). Again, this is *exponential praying*. This was not the average prayer I hear, "... if it is Your will." They prayed for boldness and I gave them exponential boldness to evangelize their Jerusalem.

Exponential praying results in *exponential boldness*. Because of their prayer meeting, "They spake the word of God with boldness" (Acts 4:31). *Exponential boldness* is witnessing to your close family members, your relatives, people you don't know, even testifying for Me to those who oppose you and object to what you say.

EXPONENTIAL PERSONAL EVANGELISM

Next, the church had *exponential personal evangelism*. The Bible says, "And daily in the temple, and in every house, they ceased not to teach and preach Jesus Christ" (Acts 5:42). *Exponential personal evangelism* is going house to house so no one misses the message. They were not just passing out tracts or church flyers. *Exponential personal evangelism* was "preaching and teaching Jesus Christ." In each home, Christians were explaining who I am and what I did on the cross.

Because of *exponential personal evangelism*, the church stepped up to a higher level of attainment, "When the number of the disciples was multiplied" (Acts 6:1). The Holy Spirit instituted a higher level of arithmetic. Previously the Holy Spirit added to My church; now He multiplies. Everyone knows the difference between adding and multiplying. If someone were to ask for money and you give them ten dollars and added another ten dollars, they might say, "Twenty dollars is not enough." Ten dollars multiplied by ten dollars is one hundred dollars. Multiplication compounds the results. That's what was happening to the church. So many people were getting saved, they were having *exponential multiplication*. What is *exponential multiplication*? When someone you win to Christ turns around to win someone else, you rejoice because they are your spiritual children and spiritual grandchildren.

EXPONENTIAL ORGANIZATION

Growth caused conflict in the early church. Some widows with Jewish names were getting bigger and better welfare than widows with Gentile names: "There arose a murmuring of the Grecians against the Hebrews, because their widows were neglected in the daily ministration" (Acts 6:1). Look what happened—*exponential organization*—this is a church continually organizing to continue evangelizing and ministering. Some churches have bureaucratic organization, which places emphasis on creating smooth-running committees and boards. But many times it is static and entrenched. Good organization always grows to accommodate winning souls and teaching My Word. A church should have *exponential organization* to

85

continually carry out the Great Commission. Rick Warren's title for a church fits this theme, *A Purpose-Driven Church.*[2] A purpose-driven church is *exponentially organized* to continually carry out the Great Commission.

What happened when the church was properly organized? The disciples gave themselves "continually to prayer, and to the ministry of the word" (Acts 5:6:4).

The next thing about *exponential organization* is that it starts at the top and works its way down. The church chose workers who were "full of the Holy Spirit, full of wisdom" (Acts 6:3). The "brethren", which meant church membership, were to find seven men who fit the spiritual qualifications, but church leadership, i.e., the pastors, had the final say, "Whom we may appoint over this business" (Acts 6:3). They wanted to continue preaching and teaching Jesus Christ (Acts 5:42).

What was the result of *exponential organization?* "The word of God increased; and the number of the disciples multiplied in Jerusalem greatly" (Acts 6:7). Exponential organization resulted in *exponential multiplication.* Previously, the church was adding new members, "now believers were multiplied greatly" (Acts 6:7)

EXPONENTIAL CHURCH PLANTING

Next was *exponential church planting:* "The churches . . . were edified; and walking in the fear of the Lord, and in the comfort of the Holy Ghost, were multiplied" (Acts 9:31). Up until now, I have been describing one church growing, i.e., the Jerusalem church. Now, new churches are being planted, "The churches were multiplied." This means *exponential church planting.*

The gospel was taken to Antioch in Syria, a heathen city. How did the believers begin witnessing? "They preached the Word to none but the Jews, only" (Acts 11:19). But then they began to witness "unto the Grecians, preaching the LORD Jesus" (Acts 11:20). This is *exponential evangelism*. When the gospel is preached to Christians on Sunday, that is expected preaching. But when you preach to the unsaved or to the heathen, then that is exponential preaching. Witnessing to people of a different race, or those living in different cultures, that is *exponential evangelism*.

Notice what happened in Antioch: "And the hand of the Lord was with them: and a great number believed and turned unto the Lord" (Acts 11:21). Again, I emphasized a great number who became Christians. This happened because of *exponential evangelism*. When people are skeptical of the validity of your message, you can use numbers to convince them of your credibility. While numbers are not the final criteria, you can use numbers because I did.

EXPONENTIAL LEADERSHIP

The church in Antioch was growing because everyone was witnessing. Then things began to really happen when they got *exponential leadership*. The report of the growth of the Antioch church came to Jerusalem, and they sent Barnabas to help the young church. What do we know about Barnabas? "He was a good man, and full of the Holy Spirit and of faith" (Acts 11:24). We know that Barnabas defended Paul in Jerusalem when no one else did. Barnabas was an aggressive leader, but when he came to this Gentile church, he became an *exponential leader*. What happened? "Much people were added unto the Lord" (Acts 11:24).

EXPONENTIAL GIVING

The next problem to face the church was a famine in Jerusalem. In your terminology, it's like a recession or a depression. So Barnabas instituted a policy of *exponential giving*. He determined to gather a large financial collection to send and help the Christians in Jerusalem. What is *exponential giving*? "Every man according to his ability, determined to send relief unto the brethren which dwelt in Judaea" (Acts 11:29). *Exponential giving* is not everyone giving the same amount, but everyone giving according to their ability. The early church continued the practice of tithing, because each believer gives a tenth of his income. Both the rich and poor give according to their income. This is called proportional giving and it is fair to all. This is also called *exponential giving* because "everyone," that means all in the church, "gave." If you really believe the message of the Great Commission that all people are lost and need the gospel, and if you really believe that I commanded you to carry out the Great Commission, then you will become involved in *exponential giving* to provide resources so that all may hear the gospel.

EXPONENTIAL FASTING

The church at Antioch was praying and fasting, "As they ministered to the Lord, and fasted" (Acts 13:2). Their prayer and fasting were successful because "The Holy Ghost said, 'Separate me Barnabas and Saul for the work whereunto I have called them'" (Acts 13:2). Thus far, the gospel had gone out, but one thing was lacking. The church didn't have a strategy to carry the gospel into all the world. They got that strategy because of *exponential fasting*. When Christians fast, they move into the area of sacrificial living. When you fast from food, you give up that which you enjoy. Also, when you fast, you give that which is necessary, because all must eat to live. So, when you fast at a certain time—one day or ten days—you are fasting and praying for Me to fulfill a certain purpose. The church at Antioch was getting ready for an *exponential strategy* that grew out of *exponential fasting*.

What does *exponential fasting* do? (a) It enables you to hear the voice of God, just as the church in Antioch heard the Holy Spirit, (b) it enables you to sacrifice (God asked the church to give up its

leadership, i.e., Barnabas and Saul), and (c) *exponential fasting* resulted in world evangelism.

EXPONENTIAL PENETRATION

When Barnabas and Saul began their missionary journey, they
might have asked, "How are we to complete the work of God in a
strange land?" The Holy Spirit told them what to do: "When they
had gone through the isle unto Paphos" (Acts 13:6). This is *exponential penetration*. They went from one end of the island to the other.
They penetrated cities, homes, businesses and lives. That's what you
must do as a strategy; you must take the gospel to every person at
every geographical place, in every area of their life. That leads to
the last principle.

SUMMARY AND CONCLUSION

Exponential evangelism is described as "using every available means
(methods) to reach every available person at every available time."
That means when you are *exponentially* reaching your town for
Christ, you have saturated every area of living and you have saturated every life. When Barnabas and Saul went through the entire
island of Cyprus, they were fulfilling the natural desire of their heart;
they were using exponential saturation.

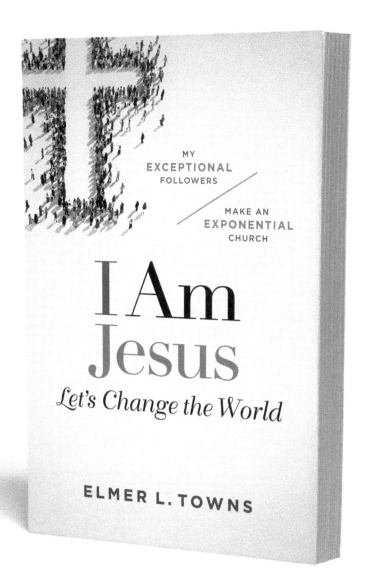

PERSONAL STUDY NOTES